Good Books books may be purchased in bulk at special discounts for sales promotion, corporate gifts, fund-raising, or educational purposes. Special editions can also be created to specifications. For details, contact the Special Sales Department, Good Books, 307 West 36th Street, 11th Floor, New York, NY 10018 or info@skyhorsepublishing.com.

Good Books is an imprint of Skyhorse Publishing, Inc.®, a Delaware corporation.

Visit our website at www.goodbooks.com.

10 9 8 7 6 5 4 3 2

Library of Congress Cataloging-in-Publication Data is available on file.

Print ISBN: 978-1-68099-320-2
Ebook ISBN: 978-1-68099-326-4

Printed in China

Let Go & Let God

A DEVOTIONAL
for Decluttering Your Heart

Ruth O'Neil

Good Books

New York, New York

Let Go and Let God

WE LIKE TO HANG ON, to hold tight to control. As we clench our grip, we may even stomp our feet and scream once in a while. But there is a better way—God's way. Before we were born, God knew exactly what each of our days would hold. Because we trust in that truth, there is nothing—no problem, no life issue— that we can't hand over to Him, relinquishing complete control.

Let go of your own ways, and let God speak to you through His Word this coming year.

The Lord is my rock and my fortress
and my deliverer, my God, my rock,
in whom I take refuge, my shield, and
the horn of my salvation, my stronghold.
—Psalm 18:2 (ESV)

In Bad Company

WE CANNOT GROW spiritually if our friends are bad influences. Are you friends with people who grumble or gossip about others? Are there people in your life who leave you in a bad mood after you've spent time with them? You don't have to drop them completely—they may need you and your good guidance. But do consider spending less time with them. We as Christians aren't immune from getting caught up in the temptation around us.

Let go of people who bring you down, and let God bring new influences into your life.

Do not be misled:
"Bad company corrupts good character."
—1 CORINTHIANS 15:33 (NIV)

Home Again

HAVE YOU EVER returned after an extended time away and found home felt different, maybe even smelled different? Oftentimes, it's not our home that has changed, but ourselves. It can feel the same when we come to know Christ. We no longer belong to the world; we just live here until He returns for us. We wait for the day when God opens His gates and says, "Welcome home!" In the meantime, we see and hear things with which we don't agree. That's as it should be—feeling out of place in this world is OK.

Let go of your ties to this world, and let God show you what He has in store in heaven.

For here we have no lasting city,
but we seek the city that is to come.
—Hebrews 13:14 (ESV)

Drop the Drama

IT'S EASY TO GET TRAPPED in competitive complaining instead of appreciating all we have. Think of all the complaining the Israelites did. God was moving them from slavery into a promised land, yet they found problems. After Cain killed Abel and God sent him away, he complained that people would want to kill him. How many people were on the earth at that time? Wasn't the entire population his immediate family? Even though Cain's complaining was senseless, God still answered and protected him.

Let go of the draining drama, and let God help you see real issues and places where you can make a difference.

"You have banished me from the land and from your presence; you have made me a homeless wanderer. Anyone who finds me will kill me!"

—Genesis 4:14 (NLT)

Ready or Not?

HAVE YOU EVER had a job that required you to complete a task beyond your current expertise? Or maybe you began a home improvement project and soon felt you were in over your head. We may feel this way in a spiritual sense, too. We may feel ill-equipped to follow a calling from God. Fortunately, if God has specifically given us a job, we already have everything we need: Him. Listen for His assignment and look for the tools God is trying to use uniquely through you.

Let go of any insecurities you may have, and let God be your strength.

It is not that we think we are
qualified to do anything on our own.
Our qualification comes from God.

—2 Corinthians 3:5 (NLT)

Big, Bigger, Biggest

EACH OF US has a different temptation, a giant that seems unstoppable. In Deuteronomy 7, the Israelites faced a sort of giant. They feared nations that were much larger than themselves. God promised them that they could overcome those nations if He went before them. But there was a warning: they needed to destroy everything. God knew that if Israel kept even some valuables, they would be tempted to fall into idol worship and fall away from God. The same can be true for us—just a little wading can send us into deep, sinful waters. Whatever our weakness, we need to keep temptation at bay with God's mighty help.

Let go of the sin that binds you, and let God help you overcome.

God is faithful, and he will not let you be tempted beyond your ability, but with the temptation he will also provide the way of escape, that you may be able to endure it.

—1 CORINTHIANS 10:13B (NIV)

Nothing to Do

IN EXODUS 35, the people served together, preparing to build the tabernacle. Everyone contributed according to their time and talents. No one cared what another person was doing. No one sat around saying, "I have nothing to offer." Afterward they celebrated. Serving Christ alongside other believers is a meaningful experience. Bring energy to a new project, group, or ministry. Find a new person with whom to serve. You will be blessed.

Let go of even just a little of your time, and let God flood your life with opportunities to serve.

And everyone who was willing and whose heart moved them came and brought an offering to the LORD . . .

—EXODUS 35:21 (NIV)

Stepping Back

WE OFTEN TAKE PRIDE in "mama bear" moves to protect our children. But at some point, we need to let them try and fail or try and succeed. We need to let them fight their own battles. Is there an area of your children's lives where you feel you need to stand on the front lines? Before charging ahead, pray and allow God to work through your child. He may reveal that you should do no more than give guidance before and love throughout the experience.

Let go of your parental leash a little at a time, and let God be the One to whom your children turn.

Listen my son, to your father's instruction and do not forsake your mother's teaching. They will be a garland to grace your head and a chain to adorn your neck.

—PROVERBS 1:8-9 (NIV)

The Rewards of Patience

JOSHUA COULD HAVE surged right into Jericho and lost that battle, but he didn't. He had patience. Even though soldiers under him likely shook their heads, Joshua waited on God and won. As in the verse below, we could all rush ahead and take over our own "cities." ("Cities" are different for each of us—they could be money, spouses, kids, in-laws, jobs, and more.) But if we are patient and listen to God, He will take care of things for us.

Let go of your impulse to take immediate action, and let God work everything out in His perfect time.

Better a patient person than a
warrior, one with self-control
than one who takes a city.
—PROVERBS 16:32 (NIV)

Look Up

THE BIBLE USES the words *flash* and *twinkling of an eye* (1 Corinthians 15:52) to describe the rapture. Before we know it has begun, it will be over. So try to picture and delight in the moment now. Some imagine that Christ's return will look like rays of sunlight reaching down to earth from the clouds. Could this vision be one of God's ways of reminding us to keep looking up? God wants us to be watchful and work to reach others for Christ with every moment we have left.

Let go of whatever turns your focus downward, and let God amaze you as you look to His return.

*Therefore keep watch, because
you do not know on what
day your Lord will come.*

—MATTHEW 24:42 (NIV)

The Face of God

THE FACE OF GOD has appeared in chips, potatoes, clouds, and more. People are looking for Christ so desperately that they look to something temporal. Christians don't need a potato chip to tell us He is real. Nature points to Him every day. You can see His hands in the gentle rain as it waters our crops, but you can also see His power in torrential rains and floodwaters. He can reveal Himself in the light whisper of a summer breeze or a stronger wind that rips up trees by the roots.

Let go of forcing your own image of Christ, and let God reveal Himself to you.

*The heavens declare the
glory of God, and the sky
above proclaims his handiwork.*

—PSALM 19:1 (ESV)

The Truth about Busyness

MOST MORNINGS, we wake up with a to-do list that is already longer than the day is. Is anything on your list unnecessary? Think about whether it's something you really want to do or something that just adds stress to your life. If it's not something God has called you to, eliminate it. You aren't required to do everything. That's the world saying you have to do it all. Don't conform to the world.

Let go of the excess busyness in your life, and let God show you the gift of life He has given you.

And let us not grow weary of
doing good, for in due season we
will reap, if we do not give up.
—GALATIANS 6:9 (ESV)

Spoiled Rotten

THERE'S A LICENSE plate frame that proclaims "Spoiled Rotten." Why would anyone want to be labeled that way? But aren't all of us as God's children spoiled rotten? We constantly sin, but God still loves us—enough to send His son to die on the cross to pay. In return, we should not only give ourselves wholly to God, but share His love with others so they can feel spoiled rotten as well. There is no greater feeling than the love of the Savior. None of us deserves Him, yet He loves us with an everlasting love.

Let go of your attempts to earn God's favor, and let God spoil you with His love.

I have loved you with an everlasting love; therefore I have continued my faithfulness to you.

—JEREMIAH 31:3B (ESV)

Light and Darkness

EVER EXPERIENCE DARKNESS so great that you couldn't tell whether your eyes were open or closed? The darkness of sin in this world can be just as overwhelming. Fortunately, there is a contrast to the darkness. There is a Light that is brighter than any sunlight. That Light is the Light of the World. God is the Light that comes into our lives the moment we accept Him. But the Light shouldn't stop there. We need to let that Light shine so everyone can see.

Let go of the darkness in the world, and let God shine His light into your soul.

God is light; in him there
is no darkness at all.
—1 JOHN 1:5B (NIV)

Which Way?

A LOT OF QUESTIONS come up in our days that need answers. Some are easy to answer and have very little impact on our lives. (What to wear? Read a book? Clean the house?) Others require much more thought and could affect many aspects of our lives and even the lives of other people. (Where to work? Where to live? Whom to marry?) God gives us assurance in the Bible that He wants to help us make decisions. We must first be listening.

Let go of all the voices telling you what to do, and let God be the voice to which you listen.

Trust in the LORD with all your heart, and do not lean on your own understanding. In all your ways acknowledge him, and he will make straight your paths.

—PROVERBS 3:5-6 (ESV)

Handle with Kid Gloves

SOME STORES KEEP their most valuable items in locked cases. If you want to take a closer look, a clerk may handle the item with white gloves to prevent oily fingerprints from ruining the piece's presentation. All the care in the world is given to a crystal bowl, but how do we care for other children of God? It's so easy to make a snide comment; we may not even realize we hurt someone. Yet the Bible tells us to lift each other up.

Let go of the way the world takes care of friends, and let God show you the proper care and value of a true friend.

Love one another with brotherly affection. Outdo one another in showing honor.
—ROMANS 12:10 (ESV)

Soaking Up the Sun

AFTER DAYS UPON DAYS of spring rain, think how good it feels to escape the gloom and doom of indoors and step outside at the first return of sunshine. Just as the warmth of the sun feels good to our skin, there is no feeling greater than that of being in the warmth of God's love. He invites us to come to Him in prayer every day. Without this time, it gets harder and harder to hear the voice of God as the commotion of the world gets louder.

Let go of the gloom and doom of the world, and let God fill you with His love.

*He dawns on them like the morning
light, like the sun shining forth
on a cloudless morning.*

—2 SAMUEL 23:4A (ESV)

Good News

OCCASIONALLY, THERE IS GOOD news in the local papers—sometimes even a story of a hero saving a stranger's life. But what about those who save people's lives from eternal damnation? Though they don't make the world's news, we know that God values and celebrates such heroes. Those heroic moments are so important to God that He actually writes the name of each one who comes to know Him in the Lamb's Book of Life.

Let go of the world's limiting view of milestones, and let God bring people into your life who need to hear His word and celebrate salvation.

They broke bread in their homes and ate together with glad and sincere hearts, praising God and enjoying the favor of all the people. And the Lord added to their number daily those who were being saved.
—ACTS 2:46B-47 (NIV)

Bare Necessities

SOMETIMES, IN ALL THE BUSYNESS, we cut out time spent with the Word. In Luke 10, we read of sisters Mary and Martha. Martha was focused on the worldly tasks she had to do. Mary wanted to sit at Jesus' feet and hear what He had to say. Martha was admonished, while Mary was praised. Devote even just ten minutes to reading the Bible. You'll find you still have time (and more energy!) to get the to-dos done.

Let go of the cares of the world for a few short moments, and let God provide you with even one verse to meditate on throughout the day.

But the Lord answered her, "Martha, Martha, you are anxious and troubled about many things, but one thing is necessary. Mary has chosen the good portion, which will not be taken away from her."

—LUKE 10:41–42 (ESV)

Adonai

WHILE JEHOVAH IS *LORD* when reading the Bible, Adonai is *Lord*. Jehovah is seen more in the Old Testament when God is dealing with the Israelites. Adonai is more prominent in the New Testament as God deals with Gentiles. The Jews are God's chosen people, but Gentiles have the same promise of salvation that God offers. It's a gift that we only need to receive. There is nothing we can do—no amount of good work, no amount of righteous living—to make him Lord of our lives. Simply accept the gift He holds out to you today.

Let go of the idea that you aren't good enough to be His child, and let God be your Adonai.

He came to his own, and his own
people did not receive him.
—JOHN 1:11 (ESV)

Faith of a Child

A FATHER AND HIS YOUNG SON were at a horse show when a man sitting near them had a heart attack. The boy watched as emergency crews gave the man CPR and took him to the hospital. As the ambulance pulled away, he asked if the man would be all right. His father wasn't sure how to respond. The boy, however, knew exactly what to say: "He'll get better if we pray for him." That boy prayed with the faith that God would answer his prayers. As adults, our minds tend to be cluttered with too many "what-ifs." We aren't sure God can handle our requests. But He can.

Let go of the "what-if" questions, and let God restore your childlike faith.

*And said, "truly, I say to you, unless
you turn and become like children,
you will never enter the kingdom of heaven."*
—MATTHEW 18:3 (ESV)

Step Out of the Courtroom

WE JUDGE just about everything—a person's appearance, date or spouse, and how they spend time and money. Most of what we judge isn't our business. More often than not, we're judgmental because people do things differently than we do. And our way is the right way, is it not? If the matter truly is important, it's an issue we need to bring before God. Should we approach the other person or let God handle it? (Although it may be difficult to believe, God probably already has it under control.) Pray about the situation and be open to God's leading.

Let go of your judgmental attitude, and let God show you if and how He wants you to act.

Judge not, and you will not be judged;
condemn not, and you will not be condemned;
forgive, and you will be forgiven.
—LUKE 6:37 (ESV)

Bird Brains

WHEN YOU CALL someone a birdbrain, it's not a compliment. God wasn't complimenting the Israelites in Jeremiah 8, either. Sometimes we can be so dense. God gives direction and we go the opposite way. If the Israelites had gone the way God told them to, their lives would have been so much easier. God laments that even the birds know what they are supposed to do and when to do it, yet His people "know not" His requirements. Is it really that we don't know, or is it that we just ignore those requirements?

Let go of foolish ideas, and let God remind you how He wants you to live.

Even the stork in the heavens knows her times, and the turtledove, swallow, and crane keep the time of their coming, but my people know not the rules of the LORD.

—JEREMIAH 8:7 (ESV)

Beyond Groundhogs

HOURS OF EFFORT go into gardening if you want productive plants. So how do you feel when along comes a groundhog to eat everything? Utter frustration at hard work gone to waste! Is that how God feels about us? He puts so much time and effort into teaching us how to live, but we fail miserably. Yet, for some reason, God continues to work with us, much in the same way we persevere in gardens to reap a much-anticipated harvest. God knows we can produce good and works to grow us into what He wants us to be.

Let go of little frustrations, and let God work His purpose through you.

Search me, God, and know my heart;
test me and know my anxious thoughts.
—PSALM 139:23 (NIV)

El Roi

ALTHOUGH GOD PROMISED to make Abram a great nation, Abram didn't think God was working fast enough. He took steps for Hagar to conceive Ishmael. Sarai then got jealous and threw Hagar and Ishmael to the curb. Hagar cried out to the Lord to be seen in her distress. We don't know if she was a willing participant, but Hagar had to live with the repercussions. You may find yourself in a similar position, feeling hurt and completely alone. Know that God sees you where you are and knows your heart. Don't wait any longer—walk into His waiting and open arms.

Let go of the hurt other people have inflicted on you, and let God be El Roi ("the God who sees me") in your life.

So she called the name of the LORD who spoke to her, "You are a God of seeing."

—GENESIS 16:13A (ESV)

Greatest Gifts

CHILDREN ARE ONE of God's greatest blessings. We nurture and care for them from their very beginnings in life. We teach them to walk and talk. Then come the days when we send them off to kindergarten, college, life. Although our roles in caring for them may change through the stages, one responsibility to them shouldn't— daily prayer on their behalf. There is no greater gift we can give them, and it's a comfort to us to know God goes with them when they walk out our door. They will never be alone.

Let go of the idea that your children will nest with you forever, and let God protect them (wherever they go) like no other can.

*Her children rise up and call
her blessed; her husband also,
and he praises her.*
—Proverbs 31:28 (ESV)

Walking in the Woods

BUILDING A HOUSE near the woods can offer protection. The tall trees provide shelter from all kinds of weather—from hot sun to driving rain and snow. Woods also can be a place to run free and explore. How much like God's protecting love! He is our refuge when we need shelter and space to just be ourselves. In fact, we can't hide from God or pretend we are someone other than who we really are. God created us—He knows us deep down inside, to the depths of our souls.

Let go of the false protection the world offers, and let God shelter you in His loving arms.

Let me dwell in your tent forever! Let me take refuge under the shelter of your wings!
—PSALM 61:4 (ESV)

The Advocate

HAVE YOU EVER acted as a go-between—an advocate—for friends, siblings, or children? It's not an easy position. Sometimes everything turns out well; other times, not so much. It's a reality of living in our broken world. But take comfort in knowing that there is an eternal advocate for us: Jesus Christ. We are born sinners, unworthy of His love and heaven, but an Advocate came and changed all that. Jesus Christ lived a sinless life yet bore our sins upon the cross. Because we have an Advocate in Jesus, we can repent of our sins and one day have a home in heaven.

Let go of trying to do everything on your own, and let God be an Advocate for you.

My little children, I am writing these things to you so that you may not sin. But if anyone does sin, we have an advocate with the father, Jesus Christ the righteous.
—1 JOHN 1:3 (ESV)

Imperfections

PIMPLES, GRAY HAIR, cellulite. . .we're masters at cover-up and camouflage. Beyond appearances, we all have deep secrets and flaws that we want to keep hidden from view. But have you ever considered how admitting your imperfections could help someone else? None of us have perfect lives, but they can be used for so much good. Pray and allow God to open doors to share your imperfections. Authenticity may deepen a relationship and also allow someone else to take a step closer to Christ. Allow God to use you when His kingdom could benefit.

Let go of hiding all your imperfections, and let God cover them with His grace and glory.

And God saw everything that he had made,
and behold, it was very good.
—GENESIS 1:31 (ESV)

Jehovah-Jireh

THE FIRST TIME we see God as Jehovah-Jireh ("the LORD will provide") is when Abraham calls Him so. God required obedience from Abraham—his son Isaac as a sacrifice. Abraham didn't know all the details; he simply obeyed and God provided a ram. We must follow Abraham's example. When God makes a request of us, we don't need to know all the where, what, how, why, and when answers. We just need to say, "Yes, God," and know that He will provide whatever it is we need.

Let go of all the questions attached to His commands and let God be your Jehovah-Jireh for the next step of your journey.

So Abraham called the name of that place, "the LORD will provide"; as it is said to this day, "On the mount of the LORD it shall be provided."

—GENESIS 22:14 (ESV)

Just Sit and Watch

EVER HAD A DAY when you wanted to pull out every gray hair you had left? Here's an idea: when children are behaving and playing nicely, just sit and watch and soak it all in. Kids will eventually feel your presence breaking the spell, so seize the moment while you have it. There won't always be squirt guns stuck in the toilet and fingerprints all over every glass surface in the house. Enjoy even those moments—and call up the memories when they've passed. The days for this time in your life are short.

Let go of all that needs to be done for just a moment, and let God show you one of his indescribable gifts—children.

Our days may come to seventy years or eighty, if our strength endures; yet the best of them are but trouble and sorrow, for they quickly pass, and we fly away.

—PSALM 90:10 (NIV)

Praying Big

ONE OF THE BEST BITS of advice you may ever receive: "Pray so big that when it happens you know it's God." Have a prayer request that seems impossible to meet in our human minds? Find a Scripture passage with a promise you need right now, and lay it all out to God. So many believers can share testimonies of prayers answered within minutes or from totally surprising places. When we come to God with sincere hearts, He will answer.

Let go of the idea that anything is out of His reach, and let God show you just how long His loving arms are.

The prayer of a righteous person has great power as it is working.

—JAMES 5:16B (ESV)

Fruitful Gardens

BOTH IN OUR GARDENS and in our spiritual lives, we can choose to let the weeds grow and take over; however, weeds will kill what good crops were trying to grow. We won't be effective witnessing tools for Christ and will bear no spiritual fruit. We need to work on our spiritual lives to get them to where God wants—a state that's useful in the work of the Lord. That task includes weeding out anything that threatens to sneak in and steal our spiritual nutrients: prayer, Bible study, worship, and fellowship with believers.

Let go of weeds in your spiritual life, and let God help you bear fruit that will glorify Him.

The LORD God took the man and put him in the Garden of Eden to work it and take care of it.

—GENESIS 2:15 (NIV)

Written on His Hand

SOME OF US are list makers. If you're not, you likely know a list maker—pen and paper always by the bed, in a purse or pocket on the go. No paper? There's always a hand. It's a habit we have in common with God. While we might jot down a task to remember or items to pick up at the store, He writes our names on His hand. That action proves how intimately He loves us and that we are in His thoughts constantly. Doesn't the idea of that just warm you all the way through with love?

Let go of thinking that you aren't important, and let God prove His love for you as you search the Scriptures.

See, I have written your name on the palms of my hands.
—ISAIAH 49:16A (NLT)

El Olam

WE LIVE IN a disposable world. Consider paper plates and paper towels. But bigger things are looked at as disposable too. If we don't like a product, or a relationship doesn't work out, we simply toss it into the trash and get a new one. Unfortunately, you may have been the one carelessly and thoughtlessly tossed aside. But take comfort: in God's eyes, you are not disposable. Our God is El Olam, the everlasting God. He will never fade away, and neither will His love for you.

Let go of the temporary things this world has to offer, and let El Olam be your everlasting God.

*Before the mountains were brought forth, or ever
you had formed the earth and the world, from
everlasting to everlasting you are God.*

—Psalm 90:2 (ESV)

Everyday Examples

PARENTS OFTEN WANT to shield children from all that's bad in the world. But sometimes unfortunate choices can be used as life lessons to show consequences. Consider an unplanned pregnancy. A secret like that can't be kept for long. Instead of trying a massive cover-up scheme, start a conversation about what can happen when we don't follow God's rules. What if the couple had been in love and married when the unexpected pregnancy occurred? The story would likely have had a happier ending.

Let go of hiding bad choices, and let God help you use them to reveal His plan for our lives.

Flee the evil desires of youth and pursue righteousness,
faith, love and peace, along with those who call
on the Lord out of a pure heart.

—2 TIMOTHY 2:22 (NIV)

The Power of Pruning

IF YOU'VE EVER toured a vineyard, you may know that growers cut the vines back so far that to the untrained eye it looks as if the plant has been killed. However, the following year the results of all that pruning are obvious in a productive plant. The grower knows which branches to prune and which to leave. God trims the spiritual branches of our lives that aren't productive to our ministry. Pruning may seem painful at the time, yet once we have gone through a growth period, we will be more fruitful than we ever could have imagined.

Let go of whatever is hindering your ministry, and let God prune areas in your life.

He cuts off every branch in me that bears no fruit, while every branch that does bear fruit, he prunes so that it will be more fruitful.

—JOHN 15:2 (NIV)

Preparing a Place

IF YOU HAD your own bedroom growing up, it probably looked quite different than your sibling's or best friend's room. Each room was unique to the child's personality. God is preparing a place just like that in heaven for us. The mansion He's building is specifically for you. God knows each of us well enough and loves us so much that He is taking time to prepare for our arrival. There truly is no greater love!

Let go of the fact that you will always be assigned to groups (family, race, religion, and so on), and let God love the individual He created you to be.

In my Father's house are many rooms. If it were not so, would I have told you that I go to prepare a place for you? And if I go and prepare a place for you, I will come again and will take you to myself, that where I am you may be also.

—JOHN 14:2-3 (ESV)

El Elyon

WE SHOULD HAVE people we can look up to, learn from, and turn to for advice. But we have a tendency to put people—celebrities, politicians, parents, children, spouses—on pedestals. The problem is, all of these people are just that. . . people, fallible people. There is only One in whom we can have faith to never fail us. That is God, El Elyon. He is the Most High God. No one can compare to Him. He is the one to whom we can look for all our needs. He is the only One who deserves to be exalted above all others.

Let go of putting your faith in fallible human beings, and let God, El Elyon, maintain the highest place in your heart and life.

That they may know you alone, whose name is the Lord, are the Most High over all the earth.

—Psalm 83:18 (ESV)

Outrageous Orders

DON'T YOU LOVE when you give children instruction and they just go and do it? No questions asked, no back talk, and no "I'll do it later." However, sometimes we give our kids impossible commands. Consider these instructions from a father to a son: "I want your room cleaned by the time I get home from work. Fold your clothes nicely and put them in the drawers. Separate your toys and put them where they belong." There's nothing completely outrageous about this request, except asking it of a two-year-old! If you wonder if you are asking kids to obey beyond their ability, teach them by working with them.

Let go of your ideas of the way everything should be, and let God show you how to gently guide and teach.

Children, obey your parents in the Lord,
for this is right.
—EPHESIANS 6:1 (NIV)

Amazing Above

HOW AMAZING IS IT that God hung the planets in space and they have been spinning in their orbits ever since? The Bible tells us many things about space that people weren't really aware of until the Protestant Reformation, when the Bible was printed and readily available to the average person. To this day, scientists are still discovering things that God has told us in the Bible. The next time Mars or any of the other visible planets can be seen, take a moment to look up and think of God.

Let go of the tendency to take the wonders of the world for granted, and let God open your eyes to see the beauty He created.

He spreads out the northern skies over empty space;
he suspends the earth over nothing.

—JOB 26:7 (NIV)

A Walk through the Orchard

DO YOU HAVE toxic relationships in your life? Some "friends" can drag us down more than they lift us up. The Bible tells us we will be known by our fruit. If we habitually hang around people content to sin, we will more than likely become like them instead of their becoming more like Jesus. Take a walk through your orchard of friends, and take note of those who bear good fruit.

Let go of any toxic relationships you may have, and let God maintain your orchard of friends.

You will recognize them by their fruits. Are grapes gathered from thornbushes, or figs from thistles?

—MATTHEW 7:16 (ESV)

To Infinity and Beyond

OUR FINITE MINDS have a difficult time trying to wrap themselves around the idea of infinity. In fact, it's almost impossible to understand. Infinite is one of God's attributes. He always was and will always be. He had no beginning and has no end. There are no limits to His strength and power, no limits to what He can accomplish. . .through you. Right now, He is writing the story of your life. God can do immeasurable things, but sometimes you need to take that first step. Don't lose heart, and don't lose hope in our infinite God. Maybe your story is just beginning. That's OK; because you're His child, He has an eternity to finish molding you.

Let go of earthly definitions and limitations, and let God, in His infinite grace, bring you everlasting life.

"I am the Alpha and the Omega," says the Lord God, "who is and who was and who is to come, the Almighty."
—REVELATION 1:8 (ESV)

· DAY 44 ·

A Wise Father

IF WE'RE HONEST, we all go through times when we feel completely inadequate to be a parent. Fortunately, we have a Father who helps each of us be the best parent we can be. When we're at the end of our rope, we can fall on our knees and leave our parenting difficulties at His feet. There, He gives us wisdom and helps us make wise decisions while raising our children through any stage—toddler and teen.

Let go of your parenting challenges, and let God give you the wisdom you need.

For the LORD gives wisdom; from his mouth come knowledge and understanding.
—PROVERBS 2:6 (NIV)

Promises, Promises

WHENEVER YOU SEE a rainbow in the sky, think of God's promises. The rainbow was God's promise to Noah that He would never flood the earth again, but the Bible is full of so many other promises. God promises salvation, protection, love, and much more—and fulfills these promises! What promises have you made to God that you haven't seen to completion? We sometimes grumble about attending church. We grudgingly give *almost* ten percent of our income. How much time do we spend in prayer? Next time you see a rainbow, also think of the promises you've made to God.

Let go of the false promises this world offers, and let God be the ultimate Promise Keeper.

Never again will all of life be destroyed
by the waters of a flood; never again will there
be a flood to destroy the earth.
—Genesis 9:11b (NIV)

Saying Sorry

HAVE YOU EVER apologized to a child? Maybe you simply lost your temper at the end of a long day or blamed him for something that you discovered in the end he didn't do. Misplaced blame can hurt, but apologies left unsaid are even more hurtful. It's good for children to see adults admitting fault and resolving tough situations. After all, we're all human. So be their example and teach them the importance of an apology.

Let go of your pride, and let God cover your wrongs with His blood.

So if you are offering your gift at the altar and there remember that your brother has something against you, leave your gift there before the altar and go. First be reconciled to your brother, and then come and offer your gift.

—MATTHEW 5:23-24 (ESV)

All-Knowing God

MOMS HAVE A GIFT. They seem to know everything their children are up to. But only God is omniscient, truly all-knowing. He knows how many hairs are on our heads. He knows us deep down into the depths of our souls. Yes, He knows the bad things, but He also knows the good. He knows the deepest desires of our hearts and the worst fears that we've shared with no one. There's comfort to be found in that. His omniscience allows us to have a relationship with Him like we can have with no other.

Let go of the worries that others will discover your deepest, darkest secret, and let God be praised for His intimate knowledge of you.

O LORD, you have searched me and known me!
You know when I sit down and when I rise up;
you discern my thoughts from afar.

—PSALM 139:1-2 (ESV)

Shades of Gray

HAVE YOU EVER heard the saying, "That's a gray area"? While there may be some gray areas in everyday life, there are no gray areas in the Christian life. We often justify our actions to make ourselves feel better. We argue that the Bible was written a long time ago and doesn't apply today. Some things are truly a personal conviction, but by searching the Scriptures, you can see what God has to say about an issue and discern whether it's truly a conviction or a command from God.

Let go of what the world says is right, and let God show you what's right in His eyes as you read His Word.

Don't you realize that all of you together are the temple of God and that the Spirit of God lives in you?
—1 Corinthians 3:16 (NLT)

Catch Them Doing It Right

A WOMAN WANTED to teach a church class for girls on appearance. The curriculum addressed the total package from the inside out. Some girls were interested; others were adamantly against it. Although they had wrong ideas about the class, they did bring up valid points. Some in the church constantly badgered the girls about their clothes, going about correction in the wrong way. We don't have any problem pointing out other people's mistakes, but we need to make a point of noticing and praising the good things more often.

Let go of looking out for other people's imperfections, and let God help you see what they're doing right.

. . . set an example for the believers in speech,
in conduct, in love, in faith and in purity.

—1 TIMOTHY 4:12B (NIV)

Talking to the Dead

MANY TV SHOWS and movies today portray the living conversing with the dead. Directors might put a humorous spin on it, but it's not funny at all. God gave the Israelites instructions that are just as pertinent today as they were then. It's amazing that people believe the dead can actually communicate with them. It only gives worldly false hope. Isaiah asks, "Why consult the dead on behalf of the living?" (Isaiah 8:19 NIV). Why would we go to someone who's dead when we have Someone who is living, just waiting for us to consult with Him?

Let go of those who promise to be a go-between with the dead, and let God be the living One you seek for every problem you might have.

Abstain from all appearance of evil.
—1 Thessalonians 5:22 (KJV)

Not Always What It Seems

AT A WOMEN'S CONFERENCE, ferns were placed in the strangest place. Knowing the men's restrooms would be called into use for women, someone had tried to pretty them up by putting ferns in the urinals. Despite the air freshener and the ferns, they were still men's bathrooms. We try to make ourselves look and smell attractive, but we can't cover up our sins. The only thing that can completely cover our sins is the blood of the Lamb. That Lamb knows exactly what we are like on the inside, yet He still loves us.

Let go of the fake cover-ups, and let God shine through, giving you true beauty.

. . . let your adorning be the hidden person of the heart with the imperishable beauty of a gentle and quiet spirit, which in God's sight is very precious.

—1 PETER 3:4 (ESV)

When God Calls You

HAVE YOU EVER tried to ignore a nudge from God? The problem is, when God gives us a job, He won't let it drop. You lose sleep. You can't get the idea out of your head. This time is when you need to focus on prayer. Even if what you need to do is painful, God will work alongside you. There is no substitute for knowing that your life story, or whatever it is God wants you to share, helped someone get through a difficult time.

Let go of the pain that keeps you from carrying out His will, and let God heal your hurt and work through your trials to help others.

Therefore, brothers, be all the more diligent to confirm your calling and election, for if you practice these qualities you will never fall.

—2 PETER 1:10 (ESV)

Purity

HELPING OUR CHILDREN stay pure for their future spouses is difficult, but we need to make a huge effort to make sure they are able. We need to teach both girls and boys to do their part and act properly. But we aren't absolved from purity as adults. We need to remain pure once we are married by not leaving question in anyone's mind about what we are doing or who we are doing it with. Paying attention to what we watch and what we read will also help keep our minds and our marriages pure.

Let go of the world's misleading ideas of purity, and let God show you His ideals.

Marriage should be honored by all, and the marriage bed kept pure, for God will judge the adulterer and all the sexually immoral.
—HEBREWS 13:4 (NIV)

Worrying or Watching?

SO MANY OF US are worrywarts. We worry about every little thing. But that's no way to live. The Bible tells us that God takes care of the smallest parts of His creation. Don't you think He'll take care of you, one of His precious children, as well? Instead of worrying, we should be watching—watching how God provides for us on a daily basis. He sends us exactly what we need exactly when we need it. It could be a word from a friend, or simply a hug from one of our children. To help yourself keep watching, start writing down these little blessings. The more you watch, the more you'll see.

Let go of your needless worry, and let God shower you with His blessings.

Casting all your anxieties on him,
because he cares for you.
—1 PETER 5:7 (ESV)

Seasons of Life

WHILE THE PHYSICAL SEASONS are enjoyable in their own way, so are the seasons of our lives. Read Solomon's description of the woman in Proverbs 31:10–31. How can any one person do all she did? She "gathered fruit in its season." Not every season of our lives is going to be entirely enjoyable, but take time to find something to praise God about during each one. Learn something from each season and pass on the wisdom you have gained.

Let go of one season when it's time, and let God show you the joy of embracing another.

There is a time for everything, and a season for every activity under the heavens.
—ECCLESIASTES 3:1 (NIV)

In the Course of Time

WHEN WE PRAY, we need to expect that God will answer our prayers. The problem comes when we treat God like a magic genie. Everything we think we want is not always good for us; it might also not be in His plans for our lives. Unlike us, God can see the big picture. He knows exactly what's to come, and He has our best interests at heart. We need to place our requests before God and allow Him to work in His own time.

Let go of thinking you know what's best for you right now, and let God answer your prayers in His perfect time.

And this is the confidence that we have toward him, that if we ask anything according to his will he hears us.
—1 JOHN 5:14 (ESV)

By Example

IF YOU GO OUT in public at all, it won't take long to see someone acting like a child—often kicking and screaming because he isn't getting his way. Paul tells us that we are to grow and put childish ways behind us. We need to learn how to deal with problems that will come up in our lives and be an example to others. Do you have someone you can emulate? Look for examples of godly people. Watch the way they handle challenging situations.

Let go of any childlike ways, and let God show you what a mature Christ follower should be.

When I was a child, I talked like a child,
I thought like a child, I reasoned like a child.
When I became a man, I put the ways
of childhood behind me.

—1 CORINTHIANS 13:11 (NIV)

Play Over

WHEN A VOLLEYBALL GAME is in play and the referee can't decide what call to make (maybe he couldn't see a play well enough), he may request a "play over." No points are awarded, no team benefits, and they just pretend it never happened. Unfortunately, in life, we don't get a play over. The decisions we make are made. But God has a solution. His blood can cover all our sins. No matter how far away we get from where we should be, we can always turn back to Him and get on the right path again.

Let go of allowing your choices to define who you are, and let God give you a play over.

Brothers, I do not consider that I have made it my own. But one thing I do: forgetting what lies behind and straining forward to what lies ahead.
—PHILIPPIANS 3:13 (ESV)

Let It Rain

WE ALL GO through spiritual times of bad weather. It may not be a huge storm. Sometimes the drizzling rain is colder, drearier, and more emotionally devastating. We may wonder why the rainy days come at all. God sends the rain so we can grow. Sometimes God sends the storms for the sole purpose of making us stop. Just as when we stay home during a storm, we may need to look within ourselves during a spiritual rain shower. We need to search the Scriptures, meditate on God's Word, and pray.

Let go of waiting out the storm, and let God show you what He has for you during the storm.

Let my teaching fall like rain and my words descend like dew, like showers on new grass, like abundant rain on tender plants.

—DEUTERONOMY 32:2 (NIV)

Masquerade's End

WHETHER AS PART of a theater production or when attending a costume party, it's fun to dress up and pretend to be someone else, even if just for a little while. But in the Christian life, there are no masquerade parties. We may try to wear a mask and hide who we really are, but God knows us through and through. We don't have to pretend with God. He knows our hearts. He knows everything we need. He knows when we're hurt and when we're happy. There is perhaps no greater comfort.

Let go of the mask you hide behind, and let God love you, warts and all.

Nothing is covered up that will not be revealed,
or hidden that will not be known.
—LUKE 12:2 (ESV)

Lost and Found

WERE YOU EVER lost in a store as a child? Or maybe one of your own children got lost? There's searching high and low, under the displays and down all the aisles. Then comes an announcement over the loudspeaker. As frightening as getting lost in a store can be, it isn't as frightening as being spiritually lost. Can you remember the smallest of details from when you accepted Christ? Or do you need to create those memories today, now? We never need to feel lost when we have that firm reminder of Whose daughter or son we are.

Let go of the enticing pulls of the world, and let God hold your hand so you will never be lost.

But we had to celebrate and be glad, because this brother of yours was dead and is alive again; he was lost and is found.

—LUKE 15:32 (NIV)

Words That Hurt

WHEN WORDS RUN rampant, we have a propensity to say things we don't mean or shouldn't say at all. People get hurt. So many friendships and families have been torn apart by gossip. While some things may be true, they don't always need to be said out loud, especially to a third party. We also need to stop gossip when we hear it begin. If a gossip doesn't have a willing ear, she will more than likely stop talking. Don't be afraid to tell someone that you don't want to participate in gossip.

Let go of the urge to talk about other people, and let God hold your tongue for you.

A perverse person stirs up conflict, and
a gossip separates close friends.
—PROVERBS 16:28 (NIV)

From Rocks to Gems

HAVE YOU EVER witnessed the rock-tumbling process? With some grinding and buffing, simple rocks transform into beautiful specimens. We too are diamonds in the rough, born with a sinful nature. However, with a little carving and shaping from God's skillful hands, we are made into beautiful gems who reflect God's goodness and love. Unfortunately, for a rock to become a gem, it must be ground down and polished. That process can be painful, but look to what you will be in the end.

Let go of the rock you are, and let God transform you into a beautiful gem.

"They shall be mine," says the LORD of hosts, "On the day that I make them My jewels. And I will spare them as a man spares his own son who serves him."
—MALACHI 3:17 (NKJV)

Shining Like Stars

THE FUNNY THING about stars is that while they are beautiful to view, they are really nothing but balls of dust and gas. Aren't we the same? Without Christ, we are nothing but dust and gas. When we accept Christ as our Savior, we become bright and shining stars, yet we have a human nature that doesn't always allow God's light to shine through. When we sin, unbelievers only see the sins we have committed. But we need to be the light of Christ shining.

Let go of anything that might be blocking the Light, and let God use you as a reflection of Him.

So that you may become blameless and pure, "children of God without fault in a warped and crooked generation." Then you will shine among them like stars in the sky.

—PHILIPPIANS 2:15 (NIV)

Coming Attractions

WHY DO WE ATTEND CHURCH? Most everyone would say it's to worship God. However, that isn't always the case. Some people expect to be entertained. Church becomes an event that needs to earn rave reviews. Church should be a place we enjoy going to. It's nice to get together with other members of the congregation and have fun—there's nothing wrong with that. The problem is when that's the only reason we go to church. Our hearts should be open to the teaching of God's Word and authentic worship.

Let go of the entertainment value church can give, and let God be worshiped in His sanctuary.

For great is the LORD, and greatly to be praised, and he is to be feared above all gods.

—1 CHRONICLES 16:25 (ESV)

Forced to Look Up

IMAGINE TAKING A WALK and catching the scent of some wonderful floral fragrance. You look to the sides of the path but don't see any flowers. About the third time you catch the fragrance, you notice purple flowers draping down from the trees. We've often heard the statement that someone has fallen so far, the only place he has to look is up. God tries to train our attention heavenward when things are going well, too. Stay open to His leading.

Let go of the distractions that keep you looking down; look up and let God reaffirm His love.

Lift up your eyes and look to the heavens:
Who created all these? He who brings out
the starry host one by one and calls
forth each of them by name.

—ISAIAH 40:26A (NIV)

More Than Scarecrows

ALL THE WORK the Israelites put into making something beautiful for worship was nothing more than a scarecrow. The people dressed up a piece of wood, but underneath, it was still a piece of wood. We too often think we're something we're not. We think we're better than other people. But God doesn't look at any one of us as better than another. It's what's in our hearts that matters to God. What's in our hearts will radiate outward and make us more than a scarecrow.

Let go of any high ideas of you have yourself, and let God be what makes you beautiful.

Their idols are like scarecrows in a cucumber field, and they cannot speak; they have to be carried, for they cannot walk. Do not be afraid of them, for they cannot do evil, neither is it in them to do good.

—JEREMIAH 10:5 (ESV)

Plant Blessings

PERENNIAL BULBS ARE favorites among flower gardeners. They need little work except for the occasional separating, because each year these flowers grow back bigger and more abundantly. In fact, many growers dig up some bulbs every few years and give them to friends. There are plenty of flowers to spread the beauty around. This kind of sharing and spreading is an example of what God instructs us to do. He wants us to be life-givers and share our food, our time, our love, our lives, and our experiences with others.

Let go of extras in your life, and let God show you where you can plant blessings for others.

The point is this: whoever sows sparingly will also reap sparingly, and whoever sows bountifully will also reap bountifully.
—2 CORINTHIANS 9:6 (ESV)

True Knowledge

HAVE YOU EVER been around people who pretend to know everything? The topic of discussion doesn't matter; they know more about it. Unfortunately, people like this also spread their lack of knowledge to biblical topics, leading astray those who are searching for the truth. We need to be on the lookout for people who fall into this camp and gently show them where they have gone wrong. We need to be careful that the sheep God entrusted to our care learn biblical truths that edify their spiritual life. Are we trustworthy, or do we speak when we have no real knowledge?

Let go of pretending you know everything, and let God teach you something you never knew before to further help others in their walks of faith.

Timothy, guard what God has entrusted to you.
Avoid godless, foolish discussions with those
who oppose you with their so-called knowledge.
—1 TIMOTHY 6:20 (NLT)

Strong to the Roots

IN A SCENE from *Little House on the Prairie,* Laura describes the prairie as wide, flat, open space. There are very few trees except for the places where there is a bit of water. Those roots grow deep. Jeremiah tells us that those who trust in God will be like those trees. We won't be just surface, Sunday Christians; our roots will go deep. We grow deep roots by securing God's Word in our hearts. It provides refreshment during difficult times. We won't have to fear when the heat comes in the form of trials. We will know God is with us, no matter what the circumstances.

Let go of anything that keeps your roots from growing deep, and let God refresh your soul with His Word.

They will be like a tree planted by the water that sends out its roots by the stream.

—JEREMIAH 17:8A (NIV)

Passing the Mantle

MOSES KNEW he wasn't going to live forever, so someone else would lead the Israelites after he died. But Moses didn't surprise Joshua with leadership at the last second; there were likely discussions over God's plans for the future. We need to train those who are coming behind us—younger Christians who need direction. God speaks through His Word, but He also speaks through us as we pass the mantle when it's time for us to move on.

Let go of the mantle you've been charged with when it's time, and let God work through another.

Then Moses summoned Joshua and said to him in the sight of all Israel, "be strong and courageous, for you shall go with this people into the land that the LORD has sworn to their fathers to give them, and you shall put them in possession of it."

—DEUTERONOMY 31:7 (ESV)

Through the Mist

A THICK MORNING MIST hides things you know are there and makes the earth seem unreal. But soon the sun burns away the fog. Until that time, lighthouses shine brightly near the ocean, guiding those out on the sea homeward. This is the way it is for those of us who live in the world. The mist is a shroud that covers what will one day be revealed by the light of Christ. The Son will rise, the mist will clear, and He will take us home to heaven. What are we doing while we are waiting? Are we helping people see that light clearly?

Let go of the fog of the world, and let God use you as a beacon to guide people home.

You are a mist that appears for a little while and then vanishes.

—JAMES 4:14B (NIV)

The Pyramid Scheme

PLENTY OF PEOPLE get caught up in pyramid schemes; they're excited to draw new people into their circle. Isn't this the way we should feel about sharing the Gospel? Unfortunately, that isn't always the case. We are comfortable with our Christianity, not excited about it. We are afraid of being embarrassed, so we don't share Christ. Imagine what it could be like if one person shared with two people, those two shared with two more people each, and so on. Soon it would be like the New Testament churches where numbers of new converts were being added on a daily basis.

Let go of worldly pyramid schemes, and let God bring meaningful returns through a revival.

And the Lord added to their number day by day those who were being saved.

—ACTS 2:47B (ESV)

Abundance

MANY FAMILIES CAN and freeze produce from summer gardens so they have plenty to eat throughout the winter. Fully stocked shelves are a beautiful sight, but sharing this abundance is so much more rewarding than keeping it all to yourself. Although sharing tomatoes or jams doesn't make us godly, it can help people see God in us. Use your abundance to open the door to sharing the Gospel with others. In that way, you will be storing up treasure in heaven, which is more important than storing up jars of food.

Let go of your stinginess, and let God use your abundance to spread His love.

Then he said to them, "Watch out! Be on your guard against all kinds of greed; life does not consist in the abundance of possessions."

—LUKE 12:15 (NIV)

Welcoming Committee

HAVE YOU EVER felt completely unwelcome? It can be especially challenging when you move and look for a new church. We all want to feel welcomed and wanted, no matter where we are. How do people feel around you? Do you reach out a warm hand in welcome, or do you pretend you didn't see them? It doesn't matter what they look like or where they come from; we need to take the initiative and be the one who welcomes them into our midst.

Let go of your inhibitions, and let God point out someone who needs you to reach out to them.

If you really fulfill the royal law according to the Scripture, "You shall love your neighbor as yourself," you are doing well.

—JAMES 2:8 (ESV)

God's Invisible Qualities

WHEW, Romans 1:20 is a big verse! But basically, Paul tells us that God's eternal power and divine nature point directly to Him. The complexities of nature are too amazing to have just happened. Why can't we just believe there is a God and that He loves us and wants us to come and live forever with Him in glory? Sin. Satan blinds our eyes and distracts us.

Let go of anything that is blocking your view, and let God reveal His divine nature.

For since the creation of the world God's invisible qualities—his eternal power and divine nature—have been clearly seen, being understood from what had been made, so that people are without excuse.

—ROMANS 1:20 (NIV)

Unknown Gods

YOU MAY NOT THINK you put your worship in anything except God, but anything that takes the place of God is an idol. Do we talk about God as much as we talk about the newest fad, phone version, TV show, beauty product, miracle diet? No matter what the latest ideas were in Athens when Paul wrote this Scripture, people haven't changed much in almost two thousand years. We still misplace our worship. That just goes to show how the Bible is as relevant today as it was when it was penned.

Let go of all the things that hinder your worship, and let God be first and foremost in your life.

All the Athenians and the foreigners who lived there
spent their time doing nothing but talking
about and listening to the latest ideas.

—ACTS 17:21 (NIV)

Five Senses

GOD BLESSED US with five senses with which to enjoy the world around us. The verse below from Philippians encourages us to use our ears and eyes to learn more about God. We need to listen to what others can teach us. We need to closely watch strong Christians. How do they act to show others the love of Christ? Look inward as well: What do others hear or see in us that could lead them to God? But just having this knowledge through the senses is not enough. We have to actually put it into practice. Having knowledge and using it are two different things.

Let go of your own understanding, and let God reveal Himself in more ways than you thought possible.

Whatever you have learned or received or heard from me, or seen in me—put it into practice.

—PHILIPPIANS 4:9A (NIV)

Sibling Against Sibling

IF YOU HAVE EVER been a sibling or a parent to siblings, you know all about sibling rivalry and the fights that can break out. How often do we get mad at our brothers and sisters in Christ? More often than not, it's just a misunderstanding. When dealing with situations like this, just remember one thing: we will all stand before God one day and be questioned on our actions.

Let go of any issues between you and another brother or sister in Christ, and let God restore your relationship.

If anyone says, "I love God," and hates his brother, he is a liar; for he who does not love his brother whom he has seen cannot love God whom he has not seen.

—1 JOHN 4:20 (ESV)

On the Other Side

OH, WHAT THE ISRAELITES had to go through before they reached the Promised Land! Disobedience forced them to walk in circles. We often have to withstand trials before we receive reward. We may know in our heads there is reward on the other side, but that knowing has yet to reach our hearts. Society teaches us that we deserve whatever we want, right now. The greatest reward that we can't always see is that, at the end, we will be stronger for having walked through the fire.

Let go of the hurry to get through your trial, and let God strengthen you during it.

Blessed is the man who remains steadfast under trial, for when he has stood the test he will receive the crown of life, which God has promised to those who love him.

—JAMES 1:12 (ESV)

Small Boats

HAVE YOU EVER been to the ocean just before a storm? Small boats are tossed around, with no control over the ocean's demands. Life is similar for new Christians. They have information coming from all directions—some confusing or conflicting. All this pushing and pulling can send a new Christian spinning out of control. To protect our family in Christ, we need to continue to grow in the Lord and be very careful about what we teach others. We certainly don't want to lead anyone down a path that leads somewhere other than to Christ.

Let go of confusing messages, and let God give you the words to share His simple message of love.

Then we will no longer be infants, tossed back and forth by the waves, and blown here and there by every wind of teaching and by the cunning and craftiness of people in their deceitful scheming.

—Ephesians 4:14 (NIV)

Have Mercy

GOD CERTAINLY IS merciful. All we have to do is look at our own sinful lives to realize He has been merciful to us by not forcing us to take the punishment for our own sins. During the plagues, God was at first even merciful to Pharaoh and the Egyptians by sparing the wheat and spelt that would ripen later in the season (Exodus 9:31–32). God showers us with mercy every day—no matter how many times we sin. We may commit the same sin repeatedly, yet when we ask for His forgiveness, God grants it. Look back on your life and see where God has been merciful to you.

Let go of any harsh attitudes, and let God help you show mercy to others.

For judgment is without mercy to one who has shown no mercy. Mercy triumphs over judgment.

—JAMES 2:13 (ESV)

No Accidents

MANY BABIES CONCEIVED in today's world are considered "accidents." Maybe it wasn't in human plans, but God had other ideas. For all of you who know you were an unplanned pregnancy, take comfort in the verse below. We were not formed in the womb just by what our parents did, but by the hand of God Himself. We all have a purpose from God in this life. Sometimes we figure out that purpose at a young age. Sometimes we spend a lifetime searching. We are not called to understand everything about life. But be assured: there are no "accidents" in God's eyes, only precious people.

Let go of the world's idea of "accidents," and let God reveal your unique purpose.

Before I formed you in the womb I knew you,
before you were born I set you apart.
—JEREMIAH 1:5 (NIV)

Open Hearts

WHEN WE READ through Exodus, we see that Pharaoh's heart kept hardening. Moses told him exactly what God was going to do if Pharaoh didn't release the Israelite slaves. Pharaoh knew, yet he ignored. Isn't that the way we are sometimes? We know exactly what God expects of us. Only it is worse with us because we are God's children; Pharaoh wasn't. When God gives us direction, we need to follow and obey immediately. The next time you feel God is telling you to do something, act. Trust God even when you can't see the outcome.

Let go of any stubbornness in your life, and let God open doors you never even knew existed.

For I know the plans I have for you, declares the LORD, plans for welfare and not for evil, to give you a future and a hope.
—JEREMIAH 29:11 (ESV)

Stagnant Water

STAGNANT WATER SMELLS and looks nasty. It attracts mosquitoes and becomes undrinkable and useless, much like the bloody water during the plagues of Egypt. Our spiritual lives also can become stagnant. We sit in a hole of depression and other negative emotions, not allowing God's light into our lives. The secret to keeping water from becoming stagnant is to keep it moving. In our spiritual lives, we need to constantly add to our knowledge of God and the Bible so we don't become stagnant.

Let go of ruts, and let God show you something new and exciting.

The LORD said to Moses, "Tell Aaron, 'Take your staff and stretch out your hand over the water of Egypt—over the streams and canals, over the ponds and all the reservoirs—and they will turn to blood.'"

—EXODUS 7:19A (NIV)

Too Much

IN TODAY'S SOCIETY it is certainly possible to have too much—but not when it comes to spiritual matters such as prayer, Bible reading, and preaching. And it's rare to hear of a surplus of money to meet needs in the church because people gave too much. But the Israelites were so faithful about giving, that is exactly what happened when they were building the tabernacle. Moses had to tell the people to stop. Wouldn't that be a wonderful thing to happen in our churches today? What a testimony to God's faithfulness that could be!

Let go of spiritual limits, and let God transform His people's time and gifts into abundance.

They are to do good, to be rich in good works, to be generous and ready to share.
—1 TIMOTHY 6:18 (ESV)

Running Out of Time

EVER FEEL AS IF there are not enough hours in the day? If time on earth is short, what are we to do? We'd better make sure we are prepared for the coming of our Lord and savior, Jesus Christ. There won't be time to get right with God then. And if we already know Christ as our savior, shouldn't we be doing all we can to make sure everyone around us knows that the return of Christ is as imminent as the changing of the season?

Let go of the thinking that you have a lifetime to accept Christ, and let God become Lord of your life today.

And God said, "Let there be lights in the expanse of the heavens to separate the day from the night. And let them be for signs and for seasons, and for days and years.

—Genesis 1:14 (ESV)

A Radiant Face

THERE ARE SOME PEOPLE who just always seem to be smiling and looking bright-eyed at the world. It's often the look of a person who knows God on a level few of us ever get to. That absolute radiance may make you think of Moses, who had to wear a veil over his face after only seeing the back of God. Imagine how he must have looked! As Christians we should be easily recognizable. Is Christ in you now? Can God's glory be seen on your face?

Let go of the struggles that make your face look downcast, and let God's glory reflect there instead.

Aaron and all the people of Israel saw Moses, and behold, the skin of his face shone, and they were afraid to come near him.

—EXODUS 34:30 (ESV)

Dressed-Up Stones

CHILDREN LOVE STONES—they see them as beautiful treasures. God also sees plain old stones as beautiful. He instructed the Israelites to build an altar using stones just the way they were, the way He created them. That's how God wants us, too, even with all our imperfections. It doesn't matter what sins we have committed; we can ask God's forgiveness. Sometimes we may feel like we have to "dress ourselves up" before we can go to God, but that isn't true. God didn't come to earth for the perfect and beautiful. He came for the bruised and broken-hearted, which is exactly what we all are.

Let go of the idea of perfection, and let God love you and use you just the way you are.

If you make an altar of stones for me, do not build it with dressed stones, for you will defile it if you use a tool on it.

—EXODUS 20:25 (NIV)

Believing without Seeing

THE DEFINITION OF FAITH is believing in something that can't be seen. We can't see God, yet we know He's there. We can't see how the sun works, yet we know it will rise again in the morning. Yet there are other areas where doubt can creep in. Are you hung up on an issue that isn't necessarily black and white? Study what the Bible has to say about that subject. Ask people who are more knowledgeable about God's Word than you. If there is not a definite answer for your question, put your faith into practice. Pray and ask God to help make it clear to you.

Let go of your unbelief, and let God speak to your heart through prayer and His Word.

Blessed are those who have not seen and yet have believed.
—JOHN 20:29B (NIV)

A Desolate Land

EVER COME UPON a place that was once a booming metropolis but is now only a ghost town? Unfortunately, this doesn't only happen in the physical places of the world; it also happens spiritually in our churches. Churches that were once thriving and living for the Lord are now lifeless. Each person in the church needs to have a relationship with both the Lord and each other. We need to lift each other up so our lives and our church buildings will no longer be desolate wastelands.

Let go of living in a barren desert spiritually, and let God bring His wonders anew into your life.

The land they left behind them was so
desolate that no one traveled through it.
This is how they made the pleasant land desolate.

—ZECHARIAH 7:14B (NIV)

Sing a New Song

WE HAVE A TENDENCY TO COMPLAIN. We don't have enough money. We don't have this or that. We hate our jobs. As children of God, we shouldn't complain. We have the love of God and forgiveness of sins. There will be times when we can feel a complaint forming on our lips, but instead of actually allowing it to come out of our mouths, let's change that complaint to praise.

Let go of the complaints that so easily spew out of our mouths, and let God put a new song in your heart.

Do all things without grumbling or disputing.
—PHILIPPIANS 2:14 (ESV)

Explained Away

EVERY FOUR YEARS we get an extra day. There are many scientific explanations as to why leap year happens, but there is also a biblical explanation. Israel was fighting a battle in Joshua 10. They marched all night but needed more time. Joshua asked that God make the sun stand still. God granted that miracle. Could that account for the glitch in our calendar? Maybe. Do scientists try to explain away a miracle from God? Often. Sometimes it's simply a miracle.

Let go of worldly scientific explanations, and let God help you see miracles.

And the sun stood still, and the moon stopped, until the nation took vengeance on their enemies. Is this not written in the book of Jashar? The sun stopped in the midst of heaven and did not hurry to set for about a whole day.

—JOSHUA 10:13 (ESV)

Fence-Sitters

TO AVOID HURTING FEELINGS or not being "politically correct," many people sit on the fence of religious and other ideas. Be assured of one thing: if you are sitting on the fence and can't decide whether or not to go the way of the cross, the Bible tells us who wins. With all the tragedies going on in the world today, it looks like Satan is winning, yet that is only an illusion. Christ will have the last word (Revelation 20:7–10). If you haven't chosen sides yet, now is the time to jump off the fence and choose Christ.

Let go of balancing on the fence on important issues, and let God give you wisdom to make the right decisions.

Do you not know that friendship with the world is enmity
with God? Therefore whoever wishes to be a friend
of the world makes himself an enemy of God.

—JAMES 4:4B (ESV)

God-Given Power

THERE MAY BE TIMES when we feel God has given us an impossible task. Never fear: when God calls us to do something, He provides the tools. When God told Moses to ask Pharaoh to free the Israelites, Moses found a roadblock each step of the way. With a little more faith, he could have seen that the tools were right in front of him. Once God pointed to the staff Moses held in his hand, Moses had no more excuses. There is nothing you can't do when you trust in the will of God and His power.

Let go of any excuses for delaying in what He has commanded you to do, and let God work His mighty power in and through you.

But he said, "What is impossible
with man is possible with God."

—LUKE 18:27 (ESV)

Hiding Out

HAVE YOU EVER been in a place in your spiritual life where you really didn't want to be? Instead of obeying God, maybe you tried to run away and hide. The only problem is, you can't hide from God. In 1 Kings 19, Elijah tried to hide out in a cave and quit his prophesying job. The only problem was that God knew where he was and told him to get back to work. We need to face the issues we were told to deal with in the first place. We can't run and hide. God always knows where we are. And that's a good thing: He promises to never leave us.

Let go of the issues that frighten you, and let God stand beside you as you face them.

It is the Lord who goes before you. He will be with you; he will not leave you or forsake you. Do not fear or be dismayed.
—DEUTERONOMY 31:8 (ESV)

Sufficient Grace

GOD SOMETIMES GIVES us trials to make us stronger. Many of these trials come so that later we may be able to help someone who is going through a similar situation. In the midst of it all, we aren't thinking of our growing faith. We just want to see a light at the end of the tunnel—and now. There are so many questions as to why God would allow it to happen. We may never know. But we can have confidence that He will get us through. He will be with us every step of the way.

Let go of the fear that you can't get through your trials, and let God be your stronghold.

But he said to me, "My grace is sufficient for you, for my power is made perfect in weakness." Therefore I will boast all the more gladly of my weaknesses, so that the power of Christ may rest upon me.

—2 Corinthians 12:9 (ESV)

Black Sheep

MANY OF US have a "black sheep" who causes an uproar in our families. Churches have black sheep as well. It's nothing new; Joshua 7 tells of sin in the camp. When the guilty sinner was discovered, he was stoned at God's command. Today, God commands us to love the sinner but hate the sin. The next time someone reveals a sin to you, don't lash out with hurtful words. Instead, be there for her. Help her overcome her faults—after all, we all have them. Let's stretch out our arms to give a hug to someone instead of throwing the first stone.

Let go of the first response of condemnation, and let God reveal how you can help restore a believer.

Better is open rebuke than hidden love.

—Proverbs 27:5 (ESV)

The Long Road

SOMETIMES IN LIFE we have to take detours. In our spiritual lives, God may give us a detour to protect us from a barrier in our path. Other times, God directs us to take the long road rather than the short road, where we can still see home tempting us to turn around and run back to its safety. The next time you feel as if you are being led down the long road, trust that God will give you the strength you need for the journey. Allow God to be your cloud as He was to the Israelites.

Let go of the shortcuts you want to take in life, and let God take you down the long road, teaching you as you walk together.

Draw near to God, and he will draw near to you.
—JAMES 4:8A (ESV)

On Your Mind

TEACHERS OFTEN TELL their students, "The mind is a terrible thing to waste." It's definitely true. Just look at the inventions that make our lives easier, better—from cars to medicine. All of these inventions started in someone's mind. Do you use your mind for the glory of God? When was the last time you meditated on a verse of Scripture from your devotions? When was the last time you woke up with the lyrics to a Christian song running through your mind?

Let go of the worldly clutter in your mind, and let God have a permanent residence there.

Finally, brothers, whatever is true, whatever is honorable, whatever is just, whatever is pure, whatever is lovely, what ever is commendable, if there is any excellence, if there is anything worthy of praise, think about these things.

—PHILIPPIANS 4:8 (ESV)

The Power of God

THERE'S A SAYING, "Never turn your back on the ocean." The water is so strong, much more powerful than we could ever be, and the waves can knock us down. The ocean is powerful because God is powerful. When we turn our backs on God, He can knock us down. There are storms of life that surprise us. But if we stand and face God, He will be with us and protect us. Then we can at least make an effort to stand as the waves of life try to knock us down, and even if we do fall, God will help us back up.

Let go of thinking you have to face life on your own, and let God prove His almighty power.

For the kingdom of God is not a matter
of talk but of power.

—1 Corinthians 4:20 (NIV)

Abandon the Anger

HAVE YOU EVER wondered why so many Christians seem angry? Often, the unhappiness comes from deep down inside when we're not following the plan God has given us. There is a battle in our souls between walking by faith and trusting God or playing it safe and living as society determines. Many Christians are not living to their fullest potential for fear of stepping out of their comfort zone and taking a risk. As children of God, we must completely abandon ourselves to Him. If we don't, we will be unhappy.

Let go of holding back and being angry, and let God direct your life.

For we walk by faith, not by sight.
—2 CORINTHIANS 5:7 (ESV)

Choices

THERE ARE A LOT OF CHOICES that come up throughout our days. It doesn't matter what questions you face today and every day to come; including God in your decision-making process is a must. And that goes for the seemingly little choices, too. You might not think God cares much about what you wear, for example, but our clothing should always be modest because we are a reflection of Christ. He wants to be involved in those bigger decisions, too. Whatever you are deciding, invite God into the process.

Let go of the false belief that you have all the answers, and let God be your guide when it comes to making decisions.

If any of you lacks wisdom, let him ask God,
who gives generously to all without
reproach, and it will be given him.

—JAMES 1:5 (ESV)

Control

WE LIKE TO FEEL in control of our lives. Without our control, we fear lack of order. Life could take us on a spin, and many things might go undone. But as much as we may like conquering chaos and checking off our lists, there are times when we need to relinquish that control. So many times in life, we have to hand over to God our spouses, our children, our jobs, or our circumstances. But here's the thing: when you hand God control of your life, it's a wonderful feeling! God has everything in His hands, so you don't have to worry.

Let go of some of the control you think you need, and let God take over.

Many are the plans in the mind of a man, but it is the purpose of the LORD that will stand.
—Proverbs 19:21 (ESV)

Nothing in Return

WHEN WE GIVE, no matter what it is, we should not expect anything in return—that's Christ's example. It feels good to help when someone needs whatever it is you have to offer: a shoulder to cry on, a listening ear, a truck to move some furniture. It doesn't need to have monetary value. You could teach a friend something she's interested in that you have know-how about.

Let go of the idea that you need payment for every kind gesture, and let God open your eyes to see who would benefit from your generosity.

But love your enemies, and do good, and lend, expecting nothing in return, and your reward will be great.

—LUKE 6:35A (ESV)

Comparatively Speaking

WHY DO WE always compare ourselves to each other? If we were all the same, the world would be boring. God purposely made us different from each other. God uses us and our personalities as we are. We need to realize that fact and be happy with where God has placed us. From now on, when you feel the thought coming, "I wish I were like. . ." stamp it out quickly. You already are exactly who God created you to be.

Let go of comparing yourself to someone else, and let God use your unique qualities for His service.

For am I now seeking the approval of man, or of God? Or am I trying to please man? If I were still trying to please man, I would not be a servant of Christ.
—GALATIANS 1:10 (ESV)

Footprints to Follow

LITTLE CHILDREN FEEL important and grown-up wearing Dad's tie or Mom's high heels. They want to be like their mothers and fathers. We need to be careful of each step we take so that when our children do follow along, they are not only following in our footsteps but in Christ's as well. God gave us these children, and we need to make sure we give them the best example. Won't it be wonderful to know that our children followed us (and God) in the way they love, share, witness, and live?

Let go of the overwhelming task of raising your children all in one day, and let God give you wisdom one step at a time.

Train up a child in the way he should go; even when he is old he will not depart from it.

—PROVERBS 22:6 (ESV)

Free to Forgive

FORGIVENESS CAN BE a very hard act of God to follow. But it's a path to freedom. When we choose to forgive someone, even if he hasn't apologized, it releases tension. We can hand the issue over to God and let Him handle it for us. When we choose not to forgive, it only hurts us, sometimes mentally and physically. Choose to forgive someone who has hurt you today and see what a difference it makes in both of your lives. You will find freedom when you truly forgive and give the situation to God.

Let go of any unforgiving attitudes, and let God bring freedom to your soul.

And whenever you stand praying, forgive, if you have anything against anyone, so that your Father also who is in heaven may forgive you your trespasses.

—MARK 11:25 (ESV)

Lay It Down

WITH ALL WE HAVE on our plates each day, why do we find it necessary to give struggles a place in our lives? Yes, life will have daily struggles. But whatever burden you face—financial, kids, marriage, job—lay it at the foot of the cross today and let God take care of it for you. It's a relief to know Someone else is taking care of things. He already knows what's on our minds and in our hearts. Put even one thing down and you will be better able to breathe.

Let go of the struggles you may be facing, and let God bear those burdens for you.

Count it all joy, my brothers, when you meet trials of various kinds, for you know that the testing of your faith produces steadfastness. And let steadfastness have its full effect, that you may be perfect and complete, lacking in nothing.

—JAMES 1:2-4 (ESV)

Change of Attitude

IF OUR WORLD is a little off-kilter, so often are our attitudes. We beg for our circumstances to change, when the truth of the matter may be that it's not our conditions but our attitude that needs changing. Examine and pray about whatever state of affairs you're in. Commit to trying to make the situation change because of your changed attitude. Work harder at becoming more like Him.

Let go of any negative thoughts about your current circumstances, and let God give you a new perspective through a change in outlook.

Therefore be imitators of God, as beloved children.
—Ephesians 5:1 (ESV)

Readjusting Our Focus

OFTEN IN OUR CHRISTIAN WALK, we get so caught up in focusing on the little things that the big things that need our attention get ignored. Those little things don't matter, yet for some reason we get stuck there. When we get stuck in one spot, we end up failing in more important areas. Ask God for direction to target what matters the most in your growth as a Christian, your service to Him, and your witness to others.

Let go of the little things in life that annoy you, and let God readjust your focus to where it truly needs to be.

I press on toward the goal for the prize of the upward call of God in Christ Jesus.

—PHILIPPIANS 3:14 (ESV)

Knowing God

ADAM AND EVE probably knew God on a level none of us will ever attain, because sin entered the world before we were born. How awesome would it be to not only hear but recognize the footsteps of our Savior! We may not be able to actually hear His footsteps, but we can feel His presence in our lives. We can talk to Him through prayer, but we need to stop and listen for Him to speak to our hearts as well.

Let go of a shallow, Sunday-only relationship, and let God be who He wants to be to you.

And they heard the sound of the LORD God walking in the garden in the cool of the day, and the man and his wife hid themselves from the presence of the LORD God among the trees of the garden.

—GENESIS 3:8 (ESV)

Reaching Out

THE GREAT COMMISSION in Matthew 28 tells us to "go into all the world and preach the gospel to every creature." That's why it's important that we don't shy away from unbelievers; instead, be an example to them. Just go slowly and withhold judgment: people don't necessarily need to hear all the "rules" for being a Christian the first time they meet you. Don't be detrimental to someone else's spiritual health; speak the truth in love.

Let go of reminding people of the rules you think they should follow, and let God convince them of what they need to change as they grow closer to Him.

You are the light of the world. A city on a hill cannot be hidden.

—MATTHEW 5:14 (NIV)

A Most Precious Gift

EVER STRUGGLE with gift giving? A woman who received a used gift claims it was the best gift ever. It was her mother's Bible. All through the Bible were notes her mom had written, along with dates. This insight into her mother's spiritual life was priceless. Another woman came into possession of her father's Bible. The pages are torn and falling out. "I know I should retire this Bible and get a new one, but I just can't!" Her father's notes on certain passages are a treasure.

Let go of any inhibitions you might have about writing in the Bible, and let God give you words to write down that might bless someone else.

The kingdom of heaven is like treasure hidden in a field. When a man found it, he hid it again, and then in his joy went and sold all he had and bought that field.

—MATTHEW 13:44 (NIV)

Praying

SOMETIMES IT'S SO DIFFICULT to pray—we feel like we don't have the will, the strength, or the words (or all of the above). However, those are exactly the times when we should be on our knees. In Romans 8:26 we read that sometimes we need to allow the Holy Spirit to pray on our behalf. What better comfort is there? God knows what our concerns are. All we have to do is be quiet and let the Holy Spirit do His work.

Let go of your normal way of praying, and let God's Holy Spirit speak for you.

...the Spirit helps us in our weakness. We do not know what we ought to pray for, but the Spirit himself intercedes for us through wordless groans.
—ROMANS 8:26 (NIV)

Choosing to Love

DOES THE VERSE below remind you of children on a playground choosing teams? When God in heaven is separating us into two groups, He looks past our athletic abilities and everything we are on the outside to see what our hearts look like. He knows who has chosen to accept Him as "Team Captain." Those who are a part of His team choose to love others, even the unlovable. Do we show that love? Have we helped others who were in need? Or did we retort to a rude person with the nastiest words we could think to say? God not only wants to be accepted by us, but for us to be available to show others His love.

Let go of any worldly ideas of love, and let God help you model real love to others.

He will put the sheep on his right and the goats on his left.

—Matthew 25:33 (NIV)

Mighty Mentors

IT SEEMS THAT GENERATIONS are often segregated from each other. The older folks sit together, the younger folks sit together. But without mixing, the younger generation misses out on learning so much—from everyday skills such as cooking and repairs to important direction on how to be a loving spouse and parent. Sometimes it's just good to have someone outside of the family circle to talk to. It doesn't matter how old you are; there is always someone who needs exactly what you have to offer. Mentoring doesn't start at any particular age. It starts when God opens the door.

Let go of the generation gap, and let God use you as a mentor or help you find a mentor of your own.

These older women must train the younger women
to love their husbands and their children.

—TITUS 2:4 (NLT)

Recognizing Gifts

WE ALL HAVE UNIQUE GIFTS within the body of Christ. Not everyone can strike up a conversation with a stranger and work God into it. Not everyone can string words together to create a story that shows God's love. Not everyone can cook a meal others want to eat. Not everyone has a background that shows a life completely changed. To find your spiritual gift, write down things you enjoy doing or skills you have. Pray for God to open your eyes and show you.

Let go of the idea that you have to be like other people, and let God show you how your gifts are unique to you.

Whatever you do, work at it with all your heart, as working for the Lord, not for human masters.
—COLOSSIANS 3:23 (NIV)

Entombed

DIFFERENT COUNTRIES, CULTURES, and religions have different customs when it comes to burying a body. Some simply bury, with or without a casket. Some burn. Some send bodies out to sea. Some cultures place not only a headstone but also a footstone. Christ's body was placed in a tomb. He had no headstone or footstone. There was only one stone at the opening of the cave, and that stone was rolled away when Christ arose from the dead. That's the only stone we need to be concerned with, because death could not keep Christ in the tomb.

Let go of the ways of the world, and let God roll away the stone that keeps you entombed in it.

Early on the first day of the week, while it was still dark, Mary Magdalene went to the tomb and saw that the stone had been removed from the entrance.

—JOHN 20:1 (NIV)

Where Are You?

THE FIRST QUESTION in the Bible is, "Where are you?" God asked Adam and Eve this question after they had given in to sin. Ashamed of their nakedness, they dressed in fig leaves and hid from God. It wasn't that God didn't know where they were; He wanted them to know where they were. God asks us the same question. Just as with Adam and Eve, He doesn't need us to answer for His benefit. He needs us to answer for *our* benefit. When we need to speak it, we focus on the answer. Are we where God wants us to be in all areas of our lives?

Let go of all the places the world says you need to be (physically and mentally), and let God place you where He needs you.

But the LORD God called to the man and said to him, "Where are you?"
—GENESIS 3:9 (ESV)

Snowflakes

SNOW: MOST PEOPLE EITHER love it or hate it. But despite what we feel about piles of snow, we can probably all agree that individual snowflakes are amazing, breathtaking. God created each one to be unique. God also created us to be unique. Sometimes we may feel ordinary or just one in a sea of faces. But in our own way, we are each amazing and wonderful and beautiful.

Let go of the feeling of not measuring up, and let God prove how wonderful and unique you are in His eyes.

I praise you, for I am fearfully and wonderfully made. Wonderful are your works; my soul knows it very well.

—Psalm 139:14 (ESV)

The Return

PART OF THE STORY of the biblical Ruth is one of waiting and watching. She essentially proposed to Boaz and then he explained that there was a closer relative who might want to marry her. Picture Ruth looking out a window, watching him walk away and wondering who, if anyone, would return. Her future was on the line. We can take a lesson from Ruth on watching and waiting. Our anticipation differs from hers in that we know our Bridegroom is Jesus Christ, and we know He is coming. But we don't know exactly when He's coming, so we should be watching and busy preparing for His return.

Let go of waiting for the world to fulfill its promises, and let God be the One for whom you watch.

She replied, "Wait, my daughter, until you learn how the matter turns out, for the man will not rest but will settle the matter today."

—RUTH 3:18 (ESV)

Jehovah

IN THE BIBLE, we see the name *Lord* often placed in all capital letters. It shows us God as "I am that I am." The Jews thought the name of Jehovah too sacred to come out of the mouths of mere humans. Today, just as in the Old Testament, Jehovah is here. He loves you. He wants to have a relationship with you. Unlike in the Old Testament, we don't need to make sacrifices or go to a priest to have our requests be made known to God. All that's necessary is you and Him and a heart that loves Him in return.

Let go of thinking that He is out of reach of mere mortals, and let God be your Jehovah.

God said to Moses, "I AM WHO I AM." And he said, "Say this to the people of Israel: 'I AM has sent me to you.'"

—EXODUS 3:14 (ESV)

Kindness in Action

A KIND PERSON is one who is sensitive to the needs of others—she not only sees but acts, usually in quiet. As one of the fruits of the spirit, kindness should be one of our notable character traits. But being kind is not always easy. We may feel that not everyone deserves our kindness. How can we be kindness in action—especially to strangers? Share a smile or greeting. Allow someone to get ahead of you in line. Compliment a server or cashier. Stop if you see someone who needs help. Our kindness in action will show others the love of Christ.

Let go of your self-conscious reservations, and let God's kindness show through you.

Be kind to one another, tenderhearted, forgiving one another, as God in Christ forgave you.
—Ephesians 4:32 (ESV)

Letting Go

WHAT WOULD YOU HONESTLY SAY if your child told you she wanted to be a missionary? To her face, you might smile and say, "That's wonderful, honey!" On the inside, however, you might begin a prayer, "Lord, please help her to change her mind. I fear for what could happen to her." Letting go of any loved one is hard. It doesn't matter how often we demand that our children stop growing; they do it anyway. When a loved one dies, the goodbye is even more painful. But, as with everything in our life, God is there for us. He knows how it feels to let go.

Let go of your fears of saying goodbye, and let God be your strength.

Behold, children are a heritage from the LORD,
the fruit of the womb a reward.

—PSALM 127:3 (ESV)

Storing Up

EVER GIVE A GIFT or share an act of kindness and not receive any thank-you in exchange? When we do things for others, if our heart is in the right place, we don't even need to hear "Thank you." When we do things in Christ's name, we are storing up treasures in heaven. And whatever treasures God has for us surely far surpass any earthly recognition.

Let go of all the blessing you think you've missed out on here on earth, and let God open the door to your heavenly treasures.

Do not lay up for yourselves treasures on earth, where moth and rust destroy and where thieves break in and steal, but lay up for yourselves treasures in heaven, where neither moth nor rust destroys and where thieves do not break in and steal. For where your treasure is, there your heart will be also.

—MATTHEW 6:19–21 (ESV)

Daughters of Defiance

GIRLS CAN HOLD SPECIAL PLACES in our hearts, whether we gave birth to them, adopted them for our own, or just borrow someone else's daughter on occasion. The two of you may have the best relationship ever. . .until that little girl gets a mind of her own. Then defiance seems to reign. No matter how bad things may get, remember that God brought that girl into your life for a reason. Ask God for wisdom in the situation. Don't be afraid to give yourself a time-out so you can step back and make a proper assessment.

Let go of any issues in your relationship, and let God grant you patience and wisdom.

Let your father and mother be glad;
let her who bore you rejoice.

—PROVERBS 23:25 (ESV)

Not Really Listening

SOMETIMES WE ASK GOD for wisdom and advice, but when He responds, we aren't really listening. Then there are the times we actually hear what God says to us, but we twist those words to get a different meaning and meet our goals. God is not against us. He only wants obedience from us. There are plenty of examples in the Bible of people who did not do as God said. None of those stories end well.

Let go of putting your fingers in your ears, and let God's truth and wisdom fill your being.

My son, if you receive my words and
treasure up my commandments with you,
making your ear attentive to wisdom and inclining
your heart to understanding; yes, if you call out
for insight and raise your voice for understanding,
if you seek it like silver and search for it as for hidden
treasures, then you will understand the fear of the
LORD and find the knowledge of God.
—Proverbs 2:1–5 (ESV)

God-Approved

IN CERTAIN OCCUPATIONS, one gets used to rejection. Consider writers and actors—they need to develop some thick skin, because rejection is all part of the job. Being rejected by people is one thing, and it does hurt. But think about how it would feel to be rejected by your Creator! Everything we do each day should be God-approved. We should always act as if God were sitting right next to us. As long as you accept Him and live your life for Him, you will never be rejected.

Let go of rejection by people, and let God's standards be a guide for your life.

Do your best to present yourself to God as one approved, a worker who has no need to be ashamed, rightly handling the word of truth.
—2 TIMOTHY 2:15 (ESV)

White as Snow

IF YOU GREW UP in certain locations, you remember praying for a snow day. You wanted it to snow like crazy overnight and into the morning but then see sun later in the day. The perfect snow day called for sledding with snow so bright it was almost blinding. Someday that's what our sins will look like. The blood of Christ will cover all the bad things we have done, washing us white as snow. It will be so bright a white we could never have imagined it.

Let go of the guilt and shame of your past, and let God wash you as white as snow.

Come now, let us reason together, says the LORD: though your sins are like scarlet, they shall be as white as snow; though they are red like crimson, they shall become like wool.

—ISAIAH 1:18 (ESV)

Cheerful Homes

THERE IS A LOT OF TRUTH to the statement, "If mama ain't happy, nobody's happy." Moms (and dads too) often set the tone for our household. No one is happy all the time (and no one should expect to be), but it is important to make the effort to have a cheerful household. When there is peace at home, everything that needs to get done will more than likely be done with a better attitude and less stress. That makes for an even happier household.

Let go of the bad parts of your day, and let God be the deep breath you need to take.

Love is patient and kind; love does not envy or boast; it is not arrogant or rude. It does not insist on its own way; it is not irritable or resentful; it does not rejoice at wrongdoing, but rejoices with the truth.

—1 Corinthians 13:4-6 (ESV)

The Next Generation

JUST LIKE THE ISRAELITES, we often neglect to pass on the knowledge of God to our children. We may focus on Bible drills and verse memorization—good tools. But what about all the times when God's presence has been real in our lives? Do you share with your children when God provided a blessing or answered prayer? How about times He has told you "No" or "Not yet"? Share it all. Teach them to recognize the love and mercies God extends.

Let go of any shyness you might have talking to your children about Him, and let God become a real part of the next generation of your family.

. . . keep your soul diligently, lest you forget the things that your eyes have seen, and lest they depart from your heart all the days of your life. Make them known to your children and your children's children.

—DEUTERONOMY 4:9 (ESV)

The Great Deceiver

DECEPTION IS literally the oldest trick in the book. Satan used deception in the Garden of Eden when he tempted Eve. Satan has been using deception ever since. He deceived Pharaoh when the magicians *appeared* to do all the same things God did through Moses with the plagues. Galatians 6:7 tells us, "Do not be deceived: God cannot be mocked." If we make a habit of studying God's Word and listening as He speaks to our hearts, we will not be deceived when the world tries to blind us to the truth.

Let go of deception, and let God be the Truth for whom you search.

He was a murderer from the beginning, and does not stand in the truth, because there is no truth in him. When he lies, he speaks out of his own character, for he is a liar and the father of lies.

—JOHN 8:44B (ESV)

Time Limits

IN NUMBERS 14 and 15, the Israelites once again doubted and disobeyed God. Only two of the spies came back and said, "With God we can take them." The other eight said, "Even God can't handle them." Their punishment was to wander around the desert for forty years. They knew at the most they had forty years to live. If you knew your days were short, how would you live your life? Perhaps you should start making changes today, because none of us is promised tomorrow.

Let go of the idea that you have a long life ahead, and let God reveal areas of your life that need your attention today.

Do not boast about tomorrow, for you do not know what a day may bring.

—PROVERBS 27:1 (ESV)

Who He Is

WHEN WE READ THE BIBLE with an open mind and heart, God never fails to reveal Himself. But in Deuteronomy 4:15–16, God did not allow the Israelites to see His face. They had a tendency to build idols. God didn't want them to create an image of Him; He wanted them to focus on who He was. We also, like the Israelites, need to focus on who He is. It is who God is that gives our life meaning and purpose.

Let go of silly notions of His appearance, and let God make known His character to you instead.

Therefore watch yourselves very carefully. Since you saw no form on the day that the LORD spoke to you at Horeb out of the midst of the fire, beware lest you act corruptly by making a carved image for yourselves, in the form of any figure, the likeness of male or female.
—DEUTERONOMY 4:15–16 (ESV)

Guidelines for Good

THE ISRAELITES WERE a stubborn people. God knew they could not live as a theocracy with just Him as their ruler. Knowing this, God set some guidelines in place for a king—including that the king should read God's Word every day. Believing in God and knowing Him through a close, personal relationship are two different things. Reading the Bible every day keeps us grounded in Him through His Word.

Let go of your busyness, and let God deepen His relationship with you.

And when he sits on the throne of his kingdom, he shall write for himself in a book a copy of this law, approved by the Levitical priests. And it shall be with him, and he shall read in it all the days of his life, that he may learn to fear the LORD his God by keeping all the words of this law and these statutes, and doing them.

—DEUTERONOMY 17:18–19 (ESV)

The Everlasting Word

GOD'S WORD IS POWERFUL and everlasting. It's a testament to the power of the Word of God to know that the Pentateuch (the first five books of the Bible) was kept with the Ark of the Covenant after Moses finished writing everything down. Most, if not all, of the sacred pieces of the temple, including the Ark itself, were lost during the captivity. But the Word of God remained. There were not several copies lying around, like the Bible in our homes today. There was only one.

Let go of any dead words and promises in your life, and let God's Word breathe life into you.

For the word of God is living and active, sharper than any two-edged sword, piercing to the division of the soul and spirit, of joints and of marrow, in discerning the thoughts and intentions of the heart.

—HEBREWS 4:12 (ESV)

Crossing the Jordan

MOSES HELD OUT HIS STAFF until all the Israelites crossed the Red Sea on dry ground. When Moses brought his staff down, the waters flowed again, drowning the pursuing Egyptian army. God performed almost the same miracle for a new generation years later, with Joshua leading across the Jordan River. When God performs a miracle, it is truly that. He leaves no room for doubt. He does the same for us. We may sometimes feel as if we're drowning in our lives. God is our life raft. We'll still need to deal with difficulties, but God will be with us.

Let go of your fear of rushing waters, and let God be the raft that brings safety and life.

But Jesus looked at them and said,
"With man this is impossible,
but with God all things are possible."
—MATTHEW 19:26 (ESV)

The World Ahead

FLOODS, HURRICANES, tsunamis, volcanoes, tornadoes, and more have been devastating to those involved. But as much as they affect our world now, these events point to a world to come. God is using these disasters to get our attention, to ready us for the reality of the coming end times. The intention is not fear but an awakening—a call to claim God as our Lord and Savior and to share the Good News with all those we meet. . .*now.*

Let go of the blinders, and let God reveal what is really going on in the world.

For nation will rise against nation, and kingdom against kingdom. There will be earthquakes in various places; there will be famines. These are but the beginning of the birth pains.
—MARK 13:8 (ESV)

A Narrow Path

PICTURE YOURSELF at a crossroads where you must choose between two paths. The narrow path is not an easy way to walk. Many people choose to walk the wider path, which is smoother and easier. But the Bible tells us the path that leads to heaven is a narrow one on which we will endure trials. Those trials strengthen us spiritually. Many distractions can get us sidetracked, so stay alert to stay on God's path. We will be rewarded once we reach our final destination.

Let go of the easy route, and let God help you navigate the narrow path.

Enter by the narrow gate. For the gate is wide and the way is easy that leads to destruction, and those who enter by it are many. For the gate is narrow and the way is hard that leads to life, and those who find it are few.
—MATTHEW 7:13–14 (ESV)

The Stubborn Weed

ONE DAY, YOU'RE WALKING along doing what you're supposed to be doing, when something reaches up and grabs you. It's a tall, stubborn weed with thorns that poke. Do you try to stamp it out or do you uproot it completely? That weed is much like the unsaved world around us that tries to keep our attention away from the things of the Lord with its sinful pokes. We must choose what we will do. We can step on it and squelch it for a little while, or we can uproot the sin and be done with it once and for all.

Let go of any stubborn sin in your life, and let God remove it completely.

. . . I am writing these things to you so that you may not sin. But if anyone does sin, we have an advocate with the Father, Jesus Christ the righteous.

—1 JOHN 2:1 (ESV)

Smooth Stones

ONE OF THE MOST RELAXING sounds is listening to a flowing creek as it runs over the stones in its bed. Years of the water flowing around and over these stones makes them smooth. In our lives, we are smoothed by the time and the experiences we go through so that we can be useful for the cause of Christ. But it takes time—just as for the stones in the creek. Look at David. Small stones were useful in conquering Goliath, in God's time and with God's help.

Let go of your impatience, and let God take as long as necessary to make your life what it's intended to be.

Then he took his staff in his hand and chose five smooth stones from the brook and put them in his shepherd's pouch. His sling was in his hand, and he approached the Philistine.

—1 Samuel 17:40 (ESV)

Resting Secure

YOUR LIFE IS ALREADY CRAZY, but you have it under control—sort of. Then something new happens that completely throws you for a loop. It forces you to let go of some activities, jobs, or responsibilities in your already overloaded schedule. At first you may see the interference as a hindrance. But take a second glance and you might find it's actually God at work. God takes our hands off of what we think is secure and moves our hands to the only true security—Him. He knows what you need, and you can rest secure in His love for you.

Let go of anything you're holding on to that lacks security, and let God be all you need.

For I, the LORD your God, hold your right hand;
it is I who say to you, "Fear not, I am the
one who helps you."

—ISAIAH 41:13 (ESV)

Disciplining Dogs

DISCIPLINE HELPS train dogs. Even after training, a dog may go to a corner and pout, ashamed (or not) of what he did. Fortunately, the mood is short lived and the dog runs back to the owner whom he knows loves him. Sometimes we too get so consumed with doing whatever it is we want to do that we forget (or not) that we should not do it. But the One who loves us will discipline us to bring our focus back. Sometimes discipline is easy and we learn quickly; other times we take a little longer to learn. Do you know why God disciplines us? Love, pure and simple.

Let go of whatever misdirects your focus, and let God's discipline be beneficial.

My son, do not despise the Lord's discipline or be weary of his reproof, for the Lord reproves him whom he loves, as a father the son in whom he delights.

—Proverbs 3:11–12 (ESV)

Picking Battles

IF YOU'VE EVER lived with a teen, you know that arguments can break over the teen's choices. Many of those choices may not be worth arguing about, when you stop and consider. However, parents do need to step in with some decisions young people try to make. God gives us many clear directions in the Bible. For example, in Romans, He tells us we should not be sexually immoral. We don't need to take every decision away from our teens, but we need to be there to guide them into making the right choices.

Let go of arguments that truly aren't important, and let God show you where to stand your ground.

All Scripture is God-breathed and is useful for teaching, rebuking, correcting and training in righteousness.

—2 TIMOTHY 3:16 (NIV)

Loving Reminders

GOD LOVES US infinitely. He puts out little reminders of His loving care for us, sometimes in the most mundane ways, throughout our days. Moms everywhere learn lessons about God's truths from the words their children innocently say. A sunset draws our attention to a beautiful and miraculous creation. God invades the lives of His children out of love. Keep your eyes open and see what little but meaningful spiritual truths God has for you today.

Let go of thinking that your daily life is mundane, and let God show you how spectacular He is.

...but the LORD was not in the wind. And after the wind an earthquake, but the LORD was not in the earthquake. And after the earthquake a fire, but the LORD was not in the fire. And after the fire the sound of a low whisper.

—1 KINGS 19:11B–12 (ESV)

First World Problems

NEVER BEFORE HAS there been so much fighting in society over trivial matters. We fight over items we want to buy as Christmas gifts. Teens fight over who gets to wear which dress to homecoming because perhaps two girls bought the same one. We fight over which phone is the best. These are First World problems. In Third World countries people don't fight over gifts; they fight to provide water and food for their families. If an opportunity arises for you to go on a mission trip, go. It will be an eye-opener for you and may help you see your "problems" in a new light.

Let go of your First World problems, and let God open your eyes.

And the king will answer them, "Truly, I say to you, as you did it to one of the least of these my brothers, you did it to me."

—MATTHEW 25:40 (ESV)

Cans versus Shoulds

LIFE IS FULL of compromises. However, there are times when we know compromise is not an option. When a girl turned thirteen, she assumed she could automatically watch all PG-13 movies. Her parents needed to help her realize that just because she was technically old enough to watch a movie didn't mean she should. There are plenty of PG-13 movies they as adults have no intention of ever watching. Our kids don't mature automatically and know that even if we can, it certainly doesn't always mean we *should*. Everything we are allowed to do as citizens of our country is not necessarily something God would be happy to see us doing, especially since our true citizenship is elsewhere.

Let go of worldly compromises, and let God show you the way of truth.

Abstain from every form of evil.
—1 THESSALONIANS 5:22 (ESV)

More, More, More

WE LIVE IN A SOCIETY of *more*. We go into debt because we want to buy more. Then we have to work more to pay off that debt. And then we wish we had more time to enjoy all the stuff. When will enough be enough? God wants us to have the desires of our hearts (sometimes), but He doesn't want us to go into debt doing it. If you are drowning in debt, consider simplifying and downsizing your life. Find ways to sell or donate some of your surplus. Cut up and cancel your credit cards. Find creative ways to save money.

Let go of "keeping up," and let God help you be a good steward of His blessings.

For we brought nothing into the world, and we cannot take anything out of the world. But if we have food and clothing, with these we will be content.

—1 TIMOTHY 6:7-8 (ESV)

Roles Are Gifts

YOU HAVE PROBABLY READ the passage of Jesus' crucifixion many times. But did you ever notice that Jesus had an aunt? Aunts can be special people in our lives. Maybe the title of "Aunt" is one you hold and cherish. We all have different roles to fill in the body of Christ. Some of us have a lot of love and understanding to give. Some are wonderful at offering an encouraging word. There are those who are always ready to feed a multitude of people at a moment's notice. Whatever your role, do it with gusto. Enjoy who you are.

Let go of trying to fill someone else's shoes, and let God put you to work where you can best fulfill a role of your own.

But standing by the cross of Jesus were his mother and his mother's sister, Mary the wife of Clopas, and Mary Magdalene.

—JOHN 19:25 (ESV)

No Longer Empty-Handed

IN THE MOVIE *Little Women*, when Friedrich Bhaer tells Jo he has nothing to offer, his hands are empty. Smiling, she puts her hands in his and tells him they aren't empty anymore. When we come before God, we have empty hands. There is nothing we can offer Him. He is the creator of the universe. We are nothing. We come to Him with our hands out, and He generously fills our hands, hearts, and lives to overflowing. When our hands are full, we should offer those blessings back to God: parents, siblings, spouses, children, job, money, homes. When we do that, we will only see more of His blessings in return.

Let go of your death grip on the blessings in your life, and let God fill your cup to overflowing.

You prepare a table before me in the presence of my enemies. You anoint my head with oil; my cup overflows.

—Psalm 23:10 (NIV)

Gold Standards

THIS WORLD IS FULL of standards. We start with standards our parents set. When we begin school, new standards follow. Our spouses have standards of what they want their partners to be. Our kids set standards to reduce the number of times we embarrass them. We set standards for ourselves. It's difficult to know on which standards to concentrate. However, there is truly only one set on which we need to focus, and those are God's standards. God loved. God served. If we focus on even just those two Christlike qualities, everything else will fall into place.

Let go of trying to live up to other people's standards, and let God be your example of a humble servant.

But emptied himself, by taking the form of a servant, being born in the likeness of men. And being found in human form, he humbled himself by becoming obedient to the point of death, even death on a cross.

—PHILIPPIANS 2:7–8 (ESV)

Seeking Justice

HAVE YOU EVER KNOWN someone who is constantly fighting for justice for the poor and downtrodden? Shouting for those who don't have a voice? She seems to have boundless energy. Consider that it likely comes from God. In all His dealings, God is just. He is fairer than we often want to be. But unlike humans, we can always trust that God will do what is right. Sometimes our views are skewed by our experiences, what we've been taught, and by human nature. As with all things, we need to search the Scriptures and pray for wisdom to discover what is right and just.

Let go of the world's idea of justice, and let God be your ruler of what is right.

At the set time that I appoint I will judge with equity.
—Psalm 75:2 (ESV)

Expanding Our Reach

WHEN SETTING UP a tent, it's imperative to pull the ropes as far as they can reach so they can be secured onto stakes. Spread out wide, these ropes and stakes keep the walls of the tent taut and standing. Loose, close ropes will not offer support. Those stakes and ropes can also symbolize our reach for God. How far is your reach? Is it contained within the four walls of your home? Do you serve in outreach opportunities? Are you involved in missions? All of those reaches are important. If your home is stable and supported, broaden your reach.

Let go of keeping Christ all to yourself, and let God direct your next step to expand your reach.

Enlarge the place of your tent, and let the curtains of your habitations be stretched out; do not hold back; lengthen your cords and strengthen your stakes.

—ISAIAH 54:2 (ESV)

One Moment

DECISIONS MADE in the moment can change lives—for better or worse. It only took one moment for Peter to deny Christ—three times. As soon as he heard that rooster crow, he knew Jesus had been right; Peter was filled with regret. But there are moments of good decisions in our lives as well. The moment you chose to accept Christ as your Savior was a wonderful one. If you haven't already made that decision, maybe right now is the moment.

Let go of making regrettable split-second decisions, and let God guide you in everything.

And Peter remembered the saying of the LORD, how he had said to him, "Before the rooster crows today, you will deny me three times." And he went out and wept bitterly.
—LUKE 22:61B-62 (ESV)

Our Solid Rock

THINK BACK TO your teenage years. Some days were over-the-top wonderful. Other days were scraping the bottom of the barrel for anything good. For most teenagers, the teen years are nothing but a tumultuous roller coaster. One of God's attributes that He didn't bestow upon us, especially as teenagers, is His immutability. God is never changing. He is the same yesterday, today, and forever. In a world where everything else around us is constantly shifting, it's comforting to know God is there and is changeless.

Let go of all the things in this world that are changing, and let God be your solid rock.

Jesus Christ is the same yesterday and today and forever.

—Hebrews 13:8 (ESV)

Fool's Gold

SOMETIMES IT'S THE LAST person you thought would do it. A friend cheats on her spouse. You can't help but think she took the gold she had and traded it for fool's gold. That is one of Satan's deceptive tricks. Yes, our spouses can be annoying some days, but so can you, sweetie. Just because our spouses might be plucking our last nerve, that doesn't give us permission to be unfaithful. Be alert. Don't get too comfortable, thinking you "would never do that!" That's when Satan will strike.

Let go of the tendency to let your guard down, and let God be the center of your marriage.

Let marriage be held in honor among all, and let the marriage bed be undefiled, for God will judge the sexually immoral and adulterous.

—HEBREWS 13:4 (ESV)

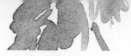

Misplaced Priorities

WE ARE ALL GUILTY of misplacing our priorities on occasion. Maybe we get caught up in a project and neglect other things that need to be done—like fixing dinner. The dilemma of misplaced priorities is not new—countless stories in the Bible tell of people not putting their focus in the right place at the right time. Think of Martha, Lazarus' sister, who was too busy preparing food to sit and listen to Jesus. David took it upon himself to move the Ark of the Covenant. His motives and heart may have been in the right place, but he didn't line up his priorities with God's, and Uzzah lost his life because of that.

Let go of what keeps you from your priorities, and let God show you what is important.

So teach us to number our days that we may get a heart of wisdom.
—PSALM 90:12 (ESV)

Jehovah Rapha

THROUGHOUT OUR LIVES we will deal with health issues, whether just a cold or something as serious as cancer. Accidents can cause injuries. Perhaps you suffer a broken heart from losing a loved one or watching someone you care about making poor decisions. Whatever the cause of your pain, rest assured that God is Jehovah Rapha, the God who heals. Sometimes healing is quick; other times, it takes much longer. Sometimes the healing doesn't come to our physical bodies but only to our spirit. Knowing God cares and understands can go a long way to healing our minds and our hearts.

Let go of your sickness and pain, hand it to Him, and let God be your Jehovah Rapha.

For I will restore health to you, and your wounds I will heal, declares the LORD.

—JEREMIAH 30:17A (ESV)

Filling the Void

WE ALL HAVE NEEDS. Sometimes when a need is not met, we feel a void. We attempt to fill that void in a myriad of ways—from buying things and working 24/7 to jumping from one unhealthy relationship to another. But these attempts will never be sufficient. We were made to worship God and have a relationship with Him. Only He can fill the void in our lives. Our hearts and lives will always have an empty space until we maintain a relationship with God. Nothing else will do.

Let go of anything you are using to attempt to fill a void, and let God consume your life.

Praise the LORD! Praise God in his sanctuary; praise him in his mighty heavens! Praise him for his mighty deeds; praise him according to his excellent greatness!
—PSALM 150:1-2 (ESV)

Walking in the Truth

PARENTS FEEL PROUD watching children make wise decisions. But then we shake our heads at other (lacking) decisions. God feels the same about us. We often know the way we should go, yet we don't always follow through. We sometimes disappoint the Lord, but He still loves us. How do we do better? Pray daily to do what is godly and right. Find godly examples for yourself. And don't dwell on what you may have done wrong in the past. When we fall away from the Lord for a time, remember how much rejoicing there is when we come back and begin anew!

Let go of discouragement over any backsliding you may have done, and let God rejoice when you return to Him and live in truth.

I have no greater joy than to hear that my children are walking in the truth.

—3 JOHN 4 (NIV)

Getting Dressed

OUR ATTIRE CAN SHOW off a bit too much—whether it's inappropriate or extravagant. It's easy to want to follow the popular trends. But even church can become a meat market or fashion show. The result: misdirected worship and the strong possibility that we're making others feel uncomfortable—whether through impure thoughts, jealousy, or feeling unworthy in their own attire. Take a moment to consider what your dress is reflecting—is it leading you or others away from God? Choose wisely, with respect for yourself and others and as a reflection of God.

Let go of dressing to attract attention, and let God show you how to clothe yourself in His wisdom.

I also want the women to dress modestly, with decency and propriety, adorning themselves, not with elaborate hairstyles or gold or pearls or expensive clothes.
—1 TIMOTHY 2:9 (NIV)

Godly Education

IN DEUTERONOMY, God commanded the Israelites to teach their children by telling them about their desert journey. We too need to make God real to our kids in our everyday lives. Going through a financial struggle? Point out how God provides for your family. Working to mend a broken relationship? Explain how God is behind any healing. When we share such experiences with our kids, they see God at work in a personal way.

Let go of the idea that education only happens in a classroom, and let God become real to your children through your teaching.

Only be careful, and watch yourselves closely so that you do not forget the things your eyes have seen or let them slip from your heart as long as you live. Teach them to your children and to their children after them.

—DEUTERONOMY 4:9 (NIV)

Short of Days

DO YOU EVER PLAY with your kids or important children in your life? Truly set aside your to-do list, let your hair down, and not worry about the mud? Take advantage of the time you have to spend with them now. Just watching movies or enjoying indoor picnics on rainy days can create special bonding moments and memories. God gave us these precious children, but the days are short. Claim them while you can. Enjoy one of God's greatest gifts.

Let go of the things that seem to need doing, and let God help you create extraordinary memories on ordinary days.

As for man, his days are like grass;
he flourishes like a flower of the field.
—PSALM 103:15 (ESV)

Choosing a Spouse

SEVERAL COLLEGE BOYS were having an amusing debate at work one night. The topic was women and what kind they wanted to marry. For the most part, the group's feelings were about the same, but there was one boy whose standards were very high. He wanted to marry a virgin. He'd had no sexual relationship with anyone, and he didn't want a wife who had. What about you? If you're single, what are you looking for in a spouse? Have you prayed for that partner? If you've already found your "one," pray for your children or single friends who might be searching.

Let go of trying to find a spouse on your own, and let God handpick the perfect mate for you.

Where you will go I will go, and where you stay I will stay. Your people will be my people and your God my God.

—RUTH 1:16B (NIV)

The Language Barrier

OFTEN, WE SAY WHATEVER we want when we're angry at one another. Even if there aren't any horrendous swear words, there is likely a lot of shouting and name-calling. This kind of language disappoints God, because of the hurt it inflicts and the wrong testimony it gives to those searching for Christ. Do you say things you don't mean to others? Our words should always be pleasing to the Lord. Don't be afraid to stop conversations when you don't like where they're going. Be a light by what you don't say, not only by what you do.

Let go of any negative talk, and let God use you to be a positive and uplifting influence.

May the words of my mouth and the meditation
of my heart be pleasing in your sight,
O LORD, my rock and my redeemer.
—PSALMS 19:14 (ESV)

In the Silence

IF YOU SOMETIMES FEEL that God is silent, you're in good company. Many people in the Bible experienced times of silence from heaven. Sarai was promised a baby, but it took thirty-seven years before that promised child came. (And God never actually spoke to her.) Jesus himself experienced silence from God as He prayed in the Garden of Gethsemane on the eve of His crucifixion. What should we do when we experience this silence? We can focus on turning away from ourselves, deepening in our dependence on Him, and seeking God's will for our life.

Let go of your self-reliance, and let God be the One on whom you depend.

To you, O LORD, I call; my rock, be not deaf to me,
lest, if you be silent to me, I become like
those who go down to the pit.

—PSALM 28:1 (ESV)

Strength in Submission

SUBMISSION IS AN IDEA that has been skewed by society. Many people believe that being a submissive wife means that you kowtow to your husband's every wish. But a submissive wife is one of the strongest women you'll ever know. She is controlled, dependable, and thoughtful. She knows how to discuss her opinions without getting overly emotional or manipulative. After making her thoughts and feelings known, she allows her husband to make the final decision for the family. If he's a godly husband, he will make the best decision possible after taking her thoughts into consideration.

Let go of the feminist idea of submission, and let God show you what biblical submission truly is.

Now as the church submits to Christ, so also wives should submit in everything to their husbands.
—Ephesians 5:24 (ESV)

The Unlovable

LET'S FACE IT: there are some people in our lives who are just difficult to love. We barely even like them, let alone love them. But our idea of love and God's idea of love are two different things. During Jesus' ministry here on earth, He hung around some pretty unlovable people. He lived yet another example for us to follow. The next time there is someone in your life who is unlovable, whether inside or outside the church family, make a point of showing her Christ's love. You may be surprised at the response.

Let go of unloving, worldly ways, and let God's love be preeminent in your life.

"The second is this: 'You shall love your neighbor as yourself.' There is no other commandment greater than these."
—MARK 12:31 (ESV)

Dumb Moments

HOW MANY TIMES does Delilah need to test Sampson before he realizes that she is trying to trick and destroy him? He acted as if he never had any clue about her treachery. His mind was not where it should have been. We do a lot of stupid things too. We listen to bad advice. We get in with the wrong people. The answer: stop, pray, and ask God for discernment. He will help you decide what to say and what not to say. He will help you discern which people in your life are true and godly friends.

Let go of those dumb moments, and let God's wisdom be part of your everyday life.

And she said to him, "How can you say,
'I love you' when your heart is not with me?
You have mocked me these three times, and
you have not told me where your great strength lies."

—JUDGES 16:15 (ESV)

Dancing Fools

WE CAN BE SO STIFF when we're worshipping, afraid to let the tears fall or lift our hands in praise. After a victorious battle, David danced down the streets of the city. His wife looked down on him with contempt. But David essentially replied that everyone should get a little foolish when praising God and that he wasn't going to change. When you worship, it should be between you and God. We need not be concerned about what people around us are thinking or doing. If you feel like shouting out, do so. If you feel like dancing like a fool, do it. God inhabits the praises of His people.

Let go of what people around you think, and let God's opinion be the only one that matters.

But thou art holy, O thou that inhabitest the praises of Israel.

—Psalm 22:3 (KJV)

Eternal, Final, Sealed

EVER WORRY ABOUT losing your salvation—or know someone who worries? Throughout the Bible there are promises of our salvation being secure. One of those passages is found in 2 Samuel 23. In *The Living Bible* translation, notice the words "eternal," "final," "sealed." David believed under the old covenant, but the security of his salvation was just the same as ours today. Search the Scriptures and you will find promise after promise that no one will ever be able to "pluck them out of" His hand (John 10:28 KJV).

Let go of any insecurities you might have about your salvation, and let God's Holy Spirit living within give you confirmation.

. . . God has made an everlasting covenant with me; His agreement is eternal, final, sealed.

—2 Samuel 23:5 (TLB)

Selah: Stop

IN THE PSALMS you may have noticed the word *Selah* appearing at the end of sentences or chapters. It means "Stop and think about it." How often do we quickly read through passages without giving them much thought? That's not what God had in mind when He had men write down His words. We are to dwell on those words, seeking their meaning. From now on, whenever you see the word *Selah*, stop, go back, and reread the passage a second or even a third time. Put some thought into it. Pause in this way with other parts of the Bible as well, not just the Psalms.

Let go of hurry when reading the Scriptures, and let God's words sink deep into your soul.

Trust in him at all times, O people; pour out your heart before him; God is a refuge for us. Selah

—PSALM 62:8 (ESV)

In Our Own Strength

WE TRY TO DO everything on our own. We are strong. . .at least, that's what we think. Abram thought he could get by on his own. So did Peter as he walked on water. But as soon as those men stopped putting their faith in God, they sank. Sometimes God allows us to come to the end of our strength. Then He patiently waits until we finally call on Him to pick us up, along with the mess we made. You can stop some of your problems from happening if you look to Christ and depend completely on Him from the start.

Let go of thinking you're the strongest person ever, and let God's arms uphold you.

Then Peter got down out of the boat, walked on the water and came toward Jesus. But when he saw the wind, he was afraid and, beginning to sink, cried out, "Lord, save me!"
—MATTHEW 14:29B-30 (NIV)

Just Believe

MANY PEOPLE HAVE tried—and failed—to disprove the Bible, Christ, and all of Christianity. The fact is, there is more proof that the Bible is true than there is evidence against it. Archaeologists often find evidence of biblical figures in Egyptian tombs and burial caves. More often than not, this evidence proves the timeline as given to us in the Bible. Look also at the many prophecies given in Scripture. Many were written hundreds of years before the prophecy was fulfilled. How could simple man have known? He couldn't, but God could.

Let go of your unbelief, and let God be proven faithful to you, even though you can't see Him.

Jesus said to him, "Have you believed because you have seen me? Blessed are those who have not seen and yet have believed."

—JOHN 20:29 (ESV)

The Blame Game

HOW EASY IT IS TO BLAME our sins on someone else. The Israelites complained that their punishment should have been someone else's. It didn't matter that God needed to send prophets such as Isaiah and Jeremiah to repeatedly warn the people to turn from their wicked ways and turn back to the Savior. They refused, and the punishment they received was deserved and for them alone. Examine your life today, and evaluate the sin in your life.

Let go of blaming others for your sins, and let God's blood, spilled at Calvary, redeem you.

Our fathers sinned, and are no more; and we bear their iniquities.
—LAMENTATIONS 5:7 (ESV)

All Sin

FOR THOSE OF YOU who have ever sinned (OK, that includes all of us!), the verse below is for you. Oftentimes we have trouble forgiving ourselves. We think whatever we have done was *so bad*, we don't believe anyone else could forgive us either. But that could not be further from the truth. You will never get so far away from God's love that you can't come back. Remember the story of the Prodigal Son in Luke 15:11–32? We are often harder on ourselves than we need to be. All we need to do is turn to God and repent.

Let go of the sin that keeps you bound up, and let God free you from its chains.

I tell you the truth, all sin and blasphemy can be forgiven.

—MARK 3:28 (NLT)

Spending Time

HOW DO YOU SPEND your time each day? Do you spend it sitting in front of the television? Do you spend a lot of time scrolling through social media? Do you spend it taking care of your home and your family? Did you take time out of your day to play with your children? Once you realize that time is a precious gift from the Lord, you will definitely spend it differently.

Let go of all the time-sappers in your life, and let God help you make the best use of time.

Go to the ant, O sluggard; consider her ways, and be wise. Without having any chief, officer, or ruler, she prepares her bread in summer and gathers her food in harvest.
—PROVERBS 6:6–8 (NIV)

Fasting as Worship

WE WORSHIP THE LORD in many ways. We sing, pray, study the Bible, and attend corporate worship. Sometimes God requires more. Perhaps you have an important decision that you need to make. We need to show God that we are serious. Fasting will help. Fasting can be skipping meals or eliminating something else from your life for a time in order to spend more time in prayer. Remember that fasting is temporary and should only be done for a set amount of time.

Let go of the things of the world that block your view of Him, and let God demonstrate how fasting can help you grow closer to Him.

And when they had appointed elders for them in every church, with prayer and fasting they committed them to the Lord in whom they had believed.

—ACTS 14:23 (ESV)

Choose to Surrender

EVER WANT TO throw in the towel? Raise the white flag? Give up? Surrender? We all have days like that. Sometimes those days stretch into weeks, months, and even years. But there is good news! In the Christian life, there is no giving up. We don't even need to carry a white flag. Surrender means realizing that we need God. This surrender is a choice. When we accept Him as Savior, we surrender to Him. When we allow Him to speak to our hearts, we surrender to Him. When we surrender our lives to Him, we give Him control. The more we surrender to God, the more intimately we will know Him.

Let go of thinking surrendering is negative, and let God go before you in everyday battles.

My son, give me your heart,
and let your eyes observe my ways.
—Proverbs 23:26 (ESV)

Just One Step

HAVE YOU EVER FELT like you were going in the wrong direction? This happens in our cars and in our lives. When this happens in our spiritual life especially, we need to make a conscious effort to change. We can't expect different results from the same steps. So take a step that heads in the opposite direction than you have already been walking. Place your faith and trust in God and allow Him to show you His plans for your life. Just one step could change everything.

Let go of taking shortcuts, and let God lead you once you take that first step toward Him.

Look carefully then how you walk, not as unwise but as wise, making the best use of the time, because the days are evil. Therefore do not be foolish, but understand what the will of the LORD is.

—EPHESIANS 5:15–17 (ESV)

True Sabbath

SABBATH MEANS "CEASING." God didn't just rest on the seventh day after He created everything in the universe; He ceased. He stopped everything He was doing. Often Sunday seems to be the day when we get all the things done that we couldn't get done during the week. We end the day just as tired as we started it. Maybe we need to give more thought to what we do on our day of rest.

Let go of the rush and hurry of society, and let God give rest to your weary soul.

Six days shall work be done, but on the seventh day is a Sabbath of solemn rest, a holy convocation. You shall do no work. It is a Sabbath to the LORD in all your dwelling places.
—LEVITICUS 23:3 (ESV)

Our Joy Is God's Joy

BECAUSE CHRISTIANS DON'T do everything the world does, nonbelievers often think that God is a hard ruler who doesn't want His children to have any fun. Many of the activities the world thinks are fun are actually sin in God's eyes. God wants us to enjoy life, and He gave us so many ways that we can. He wants us to spend hours with friends, talking about nothing and everything. He wants us to do special things with our families. As a loving Father, He gets joy out of seeing us happy.

Let go of thinking that He doesn't want you to be happy, and let God bring fun and fellowship into your life.

Behold, what I have seen to be good and fitting is to eat and drink and find enjoyment in all the toil with which one toils under the sun the few days of his life that God has given him, for this is his lot.

—ECCLESIASTES 5:18 (ESV)

God-Given Authority

MANY PEOPLE HAVE no respect for authority these days—not for parents, teachers, law enforcement officers, or government officials. But authority is God-given, whether we like it or not, and we are commanded to respect those in authoritative position. That doesn't mean we need to agree with every decision they make; they are human, after all. If there is someone in authority over you with whom you have problems, perhaps because she is an unbeliever—lift her up in prayer.

Let go of the way the world looks at authority, and let God give power to whom power is due.

Let every person be subject to the governing authorities. For there is no authority except from God, and those that exist have been instituted by God.
—Romans 13:1 (ESV)

Hide and Seek

IN JOB 23, Job's experience almost seems like a game of hide and seek. Job doesn't know where God is, and he only wants to plead his case before Him and find out why everything has happened. During the time of the Old Testament, there was no "mediator between God and man" (1 Timothy 2:5). Praise God that isn't the case anymore! All we need to do is get down on our knees and know God is there, hearing every word we utter. Because of Christ's death, burial, and resurrection, no mediator to God is necessary.

Let go of thinking He is unreachable, and let God listen to all of your prayers.

Oh, that I knew where I might find him, that I might come even to his seat!

—JOB 23:3 (ESV)

Support System

BEHIND EVERY GOOD CHRISTIAN are more good Christians. We need support that can only come from other believers. We need to have people in place whom we can call with prayer requests. Even the great King David of the Bible needed people behind him praying, fighting, and supporting him. We don't need a long list; one or two will do. Knowing you have like-minded friends behind you, supporting you and lifting you up before the throne of grace, is a feeling like no other. God promises He is among us when two or more are praying for the same cause.

Let go of going it alone, and let God provide your support system.

For where two or three are gathered in
my name, there am I among them.
—MATTHEW 18:20 (ESV)

No More Confusion

CONFUSION IS A RELEVANT word for today. People are confused about who they are. There's confusion in relationships and religion. But there should never be confusion about the Bible. Before the Protestant Reformation, people were confused religiously. They had to believe the priests on what the Bible said, because the Bible wasn't printed and readily available. When we're confused, all we need to do is grab one of the many copies we own and search for ourselves. We may need a little help understanding sometimes, but for the most part, the Bible is clear. God never intended confusion.

Let go of any confusion you have, and let God teach you through His Word.

For God is not a God of confusion but of peace.

—1 CORINTHIANS 14:33A (ESV)

Demons of Distraction

IN MANY BOOKS the main character faces one challenge after another to reach his goal. We, too, find ourselves facing multiple challenges. Have you ever known a demon named Complacency, Deception, Depression, or Fear? Those are just a few of the ways Satan distracts us from serving God. Sometimes God allows those distractions that come up in life to help us see exactly what we're made of. It's during those times we will either fail or grow.

Let go of Satan's distractions in your life, and let God cheer you on as you run the race of life.

Therefore, since we are surrounded by so great a cloud of witnesses, let us also lay aside every weight, and sin which clings so closely, and let us run with endurance the race that is set before us.
—HEBREWS 12:1 (ESV)

Why Pray?

DO YOU THINK PRAYER is useless? Maybe you wonder why anyone prays at all. We pray because it's how we speak to God. We can pray out loud, quietly to ourselves, or within our hearts if the words won't come. This world is full of people who hurt us, disappoint us, and cause us trouble. Or maybe we've caused trouble for ourselves. All of those are reasons to pray. We should pray to give thanks to God. Pray when we are repentant. Pray when we are overwhelmed and in need. Maybe a better question is, why *not* pray?

Let go of the belief that prayer doesn't help, and let God communicate with you.

Do not be anxious about anything, but in everything by prayer and supplication with thanksgiving let your requests be made known to God.

—PHILIPPIANS 4:6 (ESV)

Release the Excuses

WORLDLINESS KEEPS US from thinking we need prayer. We're busy. Guilt can keep us from praying. Some are too proud or too lazy. Some are so far away from God that they feel they can't pray. New Christians think they don't know how to pray properly. Sometimes we simply lack the faith it takes to trust in God. But God is always there. Nothing can forcefully keep us from praying. There is no magic formula. Open your heart and let the words flow. Talk to God as if He is your best friend.

Let go of all the excuses you have for not praying, and let God into your mind and heart.

I desire then that in every place the men should pray, lifting holy hands without anger or quarreling.

—1 TIMOTHY 2:8 (ESV)

What Do We Pray For?

ARE YOU AT A LOSS for words when you pray? Start by giving thanks for God's blessings. Thank Him for a beautiful sunset or for safety as you traveled. Thank Him for the hard times, too. Pray for requests friends have made, those in the midst of difficulties, missionaries, pastors, and political leaders. Pray for anyone who comes to mind—God put that thought there for a reason. Just as talking with a friend can help you see and think clearly, prayer does the same. Pray for direction.

Let go of thinking that prayer is complicated, and let God see what's truly on your heart.

Pray all the time. Ask God for anything in line with the Holy Spirit's wishes. Plead with him, reminding him of your needs, and keep praying earnestly for all Christians everywhere.

—EPHESIANS 6:18 (TLB)

Pray into Action

JOHN SMITH, THE PILGRIM, was famous for saying, "He who does not work, neither shall he eat," but he took that quote straight from the Bible. Some Pilgrims were lazy and didn't feel they had to participate in the work—at least, until they were threatened with starvation. Feeling lazy isn't bad once in a while, but we must not make a lifestyle of it as so many seem bound and determined to do today.

Let go of the habit of waiting until tomorrow, and let God help you be productive today.

Now we command you, brothers, in the name of our Lord Jesus Christ, that you keep away from any brother who is walking in idleness and not in accord with the tradition that you received from us.

—2 THESSALONIANS 3:6 (ESV)

Loving the Critic

WE AREN'T ALWAYS GOOD at accepting criticism. Some people aren't always good at delivering it. But criticism can help us see areas where we need to grow as a Christian. When it comes to criticism, we should listen quietly and reflect later. Don't lash out, but take it to heart. When you've had a chance to reflect, take the matter before God. Ask His opinion and whether it truly is something that needs work.

Let go of your defensive attitude when it comes to criticism, and let God help you see where changes in your life should be made.

The ear that listens to life-giving reproof will dwell among the wise. Whoever ignores instruction despises himself, but he who listens to reproof gains intelligence.

—Proverbs 15:31–32 (ESV)

Blessed by Ravens

HAVE YOU EVER NOTICED answers to prayer aren't always what we thought they would or should be? Sometimes those answers are downright ugly. In 1 Kings 17, God kept Elijah alive through ravens that brought him food. Not only are ravens the symbol of death in many stories, but it's a little gross that they feed off dead animals—and that's probably the meat they brought to Elijah. God will use anything it takes to get our attention. Our prayers won't always be answered in the way we wish, and blessings may come in an unappealing form. But if you look a little deeper, you'll see just how much God loves you.

Let go of thinking all good things are pretty, and let God prove how beautiful is His love for you.

... You shall drink from the brook, and I have commanded the ravens to feed you there."

—1 KINGS 17:4 (ESV)

Laughter from God

LAUGHTER IS TRULY a gift from God; it's good for the soul, a stress reliever. God wants us to laugh and be happy. On a rough day for your family, try tickling the kids just to make them laugh and relieve some of the stress you're all feeling. There's nothing quite like the sound of a child's laughter. Make a point of laughing every day, and make someone else laugh along with you. Brighten someone else's day by sending a funny picture, quote, or joke.

Let go of things that bring you down, and let God bring laughter into your life.

A joyful heart is good medicine, but a crushed spirit dries up the bones.

—PROVERBS 17:22 (ESV)

Spiritual Gifts

SPIRITUAL GIFTS ARE unique to each person. More than one of us may be hospitable, but we show it in different ways. Our gifts are determined by God. He took everything about us into consideration when He blessed us with talents. God chose our gifts, the Holy Spirit distributes our gifts, and Jesus Christ helps us work those gifts out. If you don't know your spiritual gifts, don't worry; it was never intended to be a mystery. Discover your gift by praying and serving. God will make His will known by allowing opportunities to serve come into your life.

Let go of thinking you don't have any spiritual gifts, and let God give you tasks that fulfill your personal gift.

As each has received a gift, use it to serve one another, as good stewards of God's varied grace.

—1 PETER 4:10 (ESV)

The Name of the Lord

SO MANY PEOPLE take the name of the Lord in vain today. They've become accustomed to treating the name of God as ordinary; they don't even think about it. We need to revere His name. Think about how you speak the name of the Lord. Do you spit it out flippantly, or do you speak it with the awe and reverence it deserves? This treatment is another way in which we should be different from the world. People should know how we feel; we neither speak that way nor want to hear it. If you let them know, you'll see them begin to change.

Let go of fitting in when you speak, and let God's name be solemnly spoken from your lips.

And you shall not profane my holy name, that I may be sanctified among the people of Israel.

—LEVITICUS 22:32A (ESV)

Think with God

ACTIONS HAVE CONSEQUENCES. One thing we don't think about when we act is how the consequences will affect other people. They can affect your entire family. Sometimes consequences aren't so bad; other times, they are devastating—straining relationships forever. If you are questioning what you should or shouldn't do, seriously think about any consequences there might be for you and others. Seek God's counsel to help you decide which path to take.

Let go of acting first and thinking later, and let God be part of all your steps.

For he is God's servant for your good. But if you do wrong, be afraid, for he does not bear the sword in vain. For he is the servant of God, an avenger who carries out God's wrath on the wrongdoer.

—ROMANS 13:4 (ESV)

Good Enough

UNFORTUNATELY, IT'S COMMON to feel that we aren't good enough. We feel lacking as a spouse, parent, teacher, leader, and so on. The truth of the matter is that we aren't good enough—at least we aren't good enough on our own. That's where God comes in. He knows all our weaknesses. He comes into our lives and fills the empty spaces and holes with Himself, strengthening us. Only with God are we good enough for anything. God makes up the difference when we aren't enough.

Let go of trying to be good enough in the world's eyes, and let God fill the areas in life where you lack.

But you are a chosen race, a royal priesthood, a holy nation, a people for his own possession, that you may proclaim the excellencies of him who called you out of darkness into his marvelous light.

—1 PETER 2:9 (ESV)

On the Job

WE ARE THE LIGHT of Christ wherever we go. But what happens when the environment isn't so God-welcoming? Many of us work in non-Christian environments. Some days we struggle to make it through, forced to listen to jabs made toward God and Christians. While we can choose to keep our faith a secret, the bold for Christ let everyone know where they stand. Sometimes this honesty leads to the ability to witness and have serious discussions with coworkers. We alone may not lead them to Christ, but we can allow God to use us to plant seeds in people's hearts.

Let go of hiding Christ, and let God shine through your testimony.

Nor do people light a lamp and put it under a basket, but on a stand, and it gives light to all in the house.
—MATTHEW 5:15 (ESV)

Difficult Family

DO YOU HAVE SOMEONE in your family who is hard to love? She throws your kindness back in your face. You try to be understanding, yet she constantly goes against God's ways, expecting you to be tolerant. You try to be forgiving, putting that "forgive seven times seventy" rule into play, multiple times. No matter how hard you try, nothing is good enough. How do you deal? Pray. You aren't required to hang around with them. You aren't even required to talk to them. But you do need to give them wholly to God.

Let go of the person in your life who is unlovable, and let God handle who you can't.

If anyone says, "I love God," and hates his brother, he is a liar; for he who does not love his brother whom he has seen cannot love God whom he has not seen.

—1 JOHN 4:20 (ESV)

· DAY 202 ·

Everywhere at the Same Time

GOD'S OMNIPRESENCE is a difficult concept to grasp. The thought may be creepy to a child, but to an adult, especially once we've gained a little understanding of God, it can be very comforting. It's nice to know God is with us wherever we go. At the same time, He is with missionary friends all over the world. How wonderful to know He is with our children when we can't be! It doesn't matter where you are or what you are going through: He's there. Take comfort in that today.

Let go of the idea that you can escape His eyes, and let God's presence overwhelm and consume you.

Where shall I go from your spirit? Or where shall I flee from your presence? If I ascend to heaven, you are there! If I make my bed in Sheol, you are there!

—PSALM 139:7–8 (ESV)

Waiting, Wondering, Wandering

WAITING ISN'T ALWAYS FUN. Neither is wondering. Wandering aimlessly is even worse. Did you ever doubt God? Wonder if you heard Him correctly? You aren't alone. In the Christian life there will be times of waiting, wondering, and wandering. It's what you do during those times that matters. During spiritual downtimes, focus on God, follow Him in obedience, and stay busy serving where He has already placed you. While waiting, choose a verse that applies to your situation and pray daily. Be consistent and faithful in prayer and Bible reading.

Let go of thinking everything stops when you're in a waiting period, and let God prepare you and the way He's taking you.

Wait for the LORD; be strong, and let your heart take courage; wait for the LORD!

—PSALM 27:14 (ESV)

Depend on Discernment

WHEN A FAMILY in a church asked for monetary help, members found themselves in a dilemma. It's not that the church didn't want to help, but certain members knew the issues were much deeper than lack of money to pay a bill. They took the struggle to the Lord and prayed for discernment. We need to be good stewards of the money He gave us. We don't have to give to every need that comes up. If you don't feel right about a request, seek God's guidance and He will give discernment.

Let go of handing money to everyone who asks, and let God give you discernment to know true times of need.

And it is my prayer that your love may abound more and more, with knowledge and all discernment, so that you may approve what is excellent, and so be pure and blameless for the day of Christ.

—Philippians 1:9–10 (ESV)

One-of-a-Kind

HAVE YOU EVER GOOGLED your name and found it isn't unique? Just when you think you're one in a million, you find out that you aren't. God sees you as unique. He knows every little detail that makes you . . . you. He knows the number of hairs on your head. He knows how you got that scar on your knee. He knows about the experiences that shaped you. He loves you and thinks you are truly one-of-a-kind.

Let go of thinking you aren't special, and let God show you the ways you are magnificently you and His alone.

But even the hairs of your head are all numbered.
—Matthew 10:30 (ESV)

The Bridegroom

IN LITTLE GIRLS' MINDS, everything about weddings and marriage is a fairy tale. Eventually, we grow up, reality sets in, and we realize life isn't all "happily ever after." But there is a day coming when the Bridegroom of bridegrooms will come for you. He will make all things new. He is perfect and He loves you with His perfect love. We will live with Him in glory and will never want for anything.

Let go of what this world wants for you, and let God be the Bridegroom for whom you wait.

He has covered me with the robe of
righteousness, as a bridegroom decks
himself like a priest with a beautiful headdress,
and as a bride adorns herself with her jewels.
—Isaiah 61:10b (ESV)

Playing the Victim

SO MANY OF US WANT to play the victim. Maybe you know someone who fits this description. The problem with victims is that they often can't get past the idea, and that label sticks and keeps them down so they can't move on with life. There's another label we should remember that's attached to us. It's Daughter/Son of the King. Now that's a label to talk about! Don't let other labels get you down and keep you down. If your life needs changes, decide what you can do to make things better.

Let go of worldly labels, and let God help you make a new label for who you are: victor.

Little children, you are from God and have overcome them, for he who is in you is greater than he who is in the world.

—1 JOHN 4:4 (ESV)

Rescue from Shame

WHEN WE GET IN TROUBLE as a child, we're often embarrassed and ashamed. We don't even need to be caught in our transgressions; guilt eats away at us. Shame takes over and we try to right the situation. Making everything right becomes harder when our shame is a result of more than childish disobediences. We don't need to live under the yoke of shame forever. Christ can bear it for you. Others may try to push you down and remind you of what you've done, but look to God in repentance and He will release you from all shame.

Let go of any shame you carry, and let God erase it from your record.

*As far as the east is from the west, so far does
he remove our transgressions from us.*

—Psalm 103:12 (ESV)

Misplaced Hope

"I HOPE the weather is nice this weekend." "I hope I don't get that sickness that's going around." *Hope* is a word we throw around a lot. The more we use a word, the less meaning it has, and *hope* is quickly becoming one of those words. If we thought about it, we'd realize how misplaced our hope is. Hope can be amazing if we look at it through Scripture. Jesus Christ is the only hope for this world. Unfortunately, we often look to our own power or the power of others. Don't put your hope in anything but God. He won't disappoint you.

Let go of silly hopes, and let God be all the hope you need.

May the God of hope fill you with all joy and peace in believing, so that by the power of the Holy Spirit you may abound in hope.

—ROMANS 15:13 (ESV)

Weary and Worn

MANY OF US ARE FACING overwhelming challenges. Those struggles keep us awake at night and occupy much of our thoughts during the day. It's exhausting. We aren't at our best when worries occupy our minds. We push through each day pretending we are stronger than we are, but sometimes God wants us to admit we are weary and worn. It's in that moment we speak the truth so that we can then accept the rest God offers. Being worn isn't a defeat. It's an opportunity to seek God to do something bigger than we can. You don't need to face any situation alone. With God you can overcome.

Let go of whatever struggle you face that is wearing you down, and let God help you overcome and give you rest.

Come to me, all you who are weary and burdened, and I will give you rest.
—MATTHEW 11:28 (NIV)

Keeping Up with Weeds

GARDENERS KNOW that weeds are easy to grow. They take no effort and if neglected will take over the garden. Good gardeners are in their gardens daily, eliminating the nuisances. If weeds aren't removed, the plants we want won't have a chance. When we don't give our spiritual lives the attention they need, we are neglecting God and what He wants for us and has for us to do. Weeds can be anything that take up our time and focus. Neglecting our spiritual lives keeps us from knowing God on the intimate level He desires.

Let go of neglect in any area of your spiritual life, and let God (and love for Him) bloom in your heart.

Therefore you also must be ready, for the Son of Man is coming at an hour you do not expect.
—MATTHEW 24:44 (ESV)

Walking Away

SOMETIMES WALKING AWAY is good for us. We may need to walk away from relationships, jobs, or situations in order to maintain our overall health. If you do find yourself in a time of walking away, don't be like Lot and his wife. Lot begged God to allow his family to stay in Sodom and Gomorrah. They became acclimated to unrighteous and corrupt living that was detrimental to their health. Lot finally walked away, kicking and screaming, but his wife longingly looked back, and it cost her life. If you feel like God is leading you to walk away, go. Don't second-guess, and don't look back.

Let go of what is not good for you, and let God bring you into a new place of blessing.

But Lot's wife, behind him, looked back, and she became a pillar of salt.

—GENESIS 19:26 (ESV)

Giving Ourselves

IN ORDER FOR GOD to use us, we must completely turn ourselves over to Him. That's difficult. We're selfish people. We always find time to do what we want to do, while the things of the Lord get pushed down the to-do list. When we give ourselves to God and allow Him to use us, amazing things happen. Amazing preachers of the past have reached astonishing numbers of people for Christ simply because they gave up themselves and allowed God to work through them.

Let go of yourself—your mind, talent, time—and let God do amazing things through you.

Do not present your members to sin as instruments for unrighteousness, but present yourselves to God as those who have been brought from death to life, and your members to God as instruments for righteousness.

—ROMANS 6:13 (ESV)

Our Cornerstone

JESUS CHRIST IS our cornerstone, which may seem like a strange analogy for today. A lot of technology, cement, and steel go into constructing buildings, whereas large stones and rocks used to be the basis of a foundation. A huge stone was placed at each corner of the foundation, making them the major bearers of the weight. Without strong cornerstones, the building wasn't sure. We need a cornerstone. Without Christ, we have no foundation. If we don't believe He left heaven to come to earth to be born of a virgin, died on the cross for our sins, was buried, and rose again, we have nothing.

Let go of anything that promises to give you support, and let God be your true cornerstone.

This Jesus is the stone that was rejected by you, the builders, which has become the cornerstone.

—ACTS 4:11 (ESV)

Allowing God's Blessings

EVER KNOW SOMEONE who is constantly finding some new reason to be jealous? But what people like this often don't realize is that God has blessings waiting for them; they just aren't where they need to be to receive those blessings. They're too busy worrying over someone else to see their own blessings. While they may focus on monetary blessings, they miss out on so many other blessings God has for them. Open your eyes to see His blessings to you.

Let go of any jealousy you might have of other people's blessings, and let God fill your hands with blessings specifically for you.

Give, and it will be given to you. Good measure, pressed down, shaken together, running over, will be put into your lap. For with the measure you use it will be measured back to you.
—LUKE 6:38 (ESV)

Music for the Soul

MUSIC CAN BE emotional, even bringing us to tears. When's the last time a combination of words and music allowed you to want to simply bask in the goodness and glory of God? When's the last time the music you listened to music pointed to God? Change the station and listen to music that worships the Creator. Turn the volume up loud. Close your eyes, listen to the words, and absorb the music itself. Take it all in.

Let go of the music of the world, and let God be worshiped deep down in your soul.

*Praise him with trumpet sound; praise
him with lute and harp! Praise him with
tambourine and dance; praise him with strings
and pipe! Praise him with sounding cymbals;
praise him with loud clashing cymbals!*

—Psalm 150:3–5 (ESV)

Enjoy the Differences

IS THERE SOMEONE in your family whom you resemble in appearance yet is very different than you in other ways? Our brothers and sisters in Christ may be different in ways we don't at first think are complementary, but we need to celebrate those differences. We need to celebrate the imagination of a wonderful Creator. Don't try to change others; instead, celebrate that you are not a carbon copy. God made us unique for a reason.

Let go of thinking everyone should be like you, and let God show you how wonderful differences can be.

As it is, there are many parts, yet one body.
—1 CORINTHIANS 12:20 (ESV)

Righteous Living

TODAY IS A DAY OF TOLERANCE. At every turn we are encouraged or even commanded to be tolerant of everyone's ideas and lifestyles. Unfortunately, not all those ideas and lifestyles are righteous. Many people who live in sin feel persecuted when Christians don't agree with their way of life. They bark at us, saying we are intolerant. But they are not tolerant or understanding of our views and beliefs. The Bible tells us to be ready to answer for what we believe. If you are dealing with someone who expects tolerance of you, search the Scriptures for answers.

Let go of all that the world says about how to live life, and let God speak to you through His Word.

Preach the word; be ready in season and out of season; reprove, rebuke, and exhort, with complete patience and teaching.

—2 TIMOTHY 4:2 (ESV)

Chasing Jesus

WE DO A LOT OF CHASING throughout the day. We chase our kids. Sometimes we chase relationships, wealth, fame, the clock. All that running leaves us tired. The problem comes when we as Christians don't chase after God. God blesses us beyond measure; the least we could do is seek Him. Any dreams we have for our lives, even fulfilled ones, will be empty and unsatisfying if we aren't chasing Jesus. Our life will have no purpose. Any enjoyment we experience from the things we chase will be temporary if Christ isn't a priority. Jesus cannot fail us, and He is where true satisfaction is.

Let go of the rat race you are running, and let God be the one you chase.

Seek the LORD while he may be found;
call upon him while he is near.

—ISAIAH 55:6 (ESV)

Powerful Hands

HANDS ARE ONE of the busiest parts of the body. They work, show love, hold, and comfort. You can tell a lot about a person by looking at his hands—beyond the type of work he does. You can learn by watching mannerisms and movements how he treats people. Jesus' hands were nailed to the cross for us. Those impaled hands held the weight of the sin of the entire world. Thomas, one of the disciples, would not believe Jesus had risen from the grave until he saw the nail-pierced hands for Himself.

Let go of the weight of your world, and let God's hand bear it for you.

So the other disciples told him, "We have seen the Lord." But he said to them, "Unless I see in his hands the mark of the nails, and place my finger into the mark of the nails, and place my hand into his side, I will never believe."

—JOHN 20:25 (ESV)

No Middle Ground

HERE'S A PROFOUND THOUGHT: you can either be a disciple of Christ or a pawn of Satan. There is no middle ground, and there is no third option. We cannot be indifferent in our spiritual thoughts and lives. We must be wholly committed to Christ. When we are indifferent, our testimony has little value. Unbelievers won't see us as any different than the rest of the world. Many believe that if they are good people, that's enough. But it's not. Maybe you've been a little lukewarm in your spirituality. Remember, by not choosing, you have chosen, and you will find yourself aligned with the wrong side. That's a dangerous place to be.

Let go of your lukewarm attitude, and let God heat up the passion with which you live for Him.

So, because you are lukewarm, and neither hot nor cold, I will spit you out of my mouth.

—Revelation 3:16 (ESV)

Priceless Lessons

HINDSIGHT IS 20/20. We can all look back on our lives and see where we should have done things differently. The reverse is also true: we can look back and see where we did things right. Sometimes we can see where God was at work in our lives, preparing or teaching us. These life lessons from God are priceless gifts. Recall some of the difficulties you've been through. See how God used them for your good for His glory. Have you changed because of His work in you?

Let go of thinking that all bad times are simply bad, and let God show you how far you've come.

And we know that for those who love God all things work together for good, for those who are called according to his purpose.

—ROMANS 8:28 (ESV)

The Messiah

MESSIAH MEANS "PROMISED ONE." Throughout time people have proclaimed to be a messiah. Jesus is the one true Messiah, but when He revealed who He was, people didn't believe Him. At that time, some people weren't looking for a messiah at all, and some were looking for a messiah in the wrong place. Even today, some people are still looking for a messiah to come and save them. But the Messiah has already come. He has already paid the price for our sin, and He is returning for those who love Him.

Let go of looking for a messiah to come into your life, and let God show you He already has.

The woman said to him, "I know that Messiah is coming (he who is called Christ). When he comes, he will tell us all things." Jesus said to her, "I who speak to you am he."

—JOHN 4:25–26 (ESV)

Perfect Parent

THE PERFECT PARENT? There are no perfect parents, only parents who are perfect for the children God gave them. Some days we think we have this parenting thing figured out, but then we realize we haven't figured out anything. Sometimes we make good decisions, and other times. . . God never intended us for us to walk the parenting path alone. He gives us instructions in the Bible, and we can go to Him in prayer when we need guidance. We may never achieve the status of being a perfect parent, but we can be loving, and that could make all the difference for your child.

Let go of trying to obtain perfection, and let God help you be the parent your kids need.

*Behold, children are a heritage from the LORD,
the fruit of the womb a reward.*

—PSALM 127:3 (ESV)

The Reach of Our Testimony

THE BIBLICAL DANIEL was just a teenager when he was taken captive to Babylon and was kept there until he was an old man. He made an impression early on when he refused to eat the king's rich food, requesting only vegetables and water. He continued making impressions throughout the reigns of four different kings. We may never be able to have the influence of Daniel, but our testimony can still reach future generations. You must share your story with others. There is someone—maybe even someone not yet born—who needs to hear.

Let go of keeping your testimony to yourself, and let God spread your reach wide.

"Return to your home, and declare how much God has done for you."

—LUKE 8:39A (ESV)

A Lesson from Rahab

GOD CAN USE YOU to bless anyone. Need proof? Rahab. Rahab wasn't a Jew. She was a citizen of Jericho, a prostitute. That didn't matter. She'd heard rumors of the Israelites annihilating everyone in their path. She feared they would one day come to destroy her home. When she heard they had Jericho in their sights, she did what she could to save herself and her family by protecting Israelite spies. God used her and then blessed her faith by moving her into the genealogical line of Christ.

Let go of thinking you are nothing and that He can't use you, and let God bless others while working through you.

By faith the prostitute Rahab, because she welcomed the spies, was not killed with those who were disobedient.

—HEBREWS 11:31 (NIV)

Noise of the World

DON'T YOU WISH you could wear noise-canceling headphones all the time? This world gets to be quite the noisy place. So many voices come at us from all different directions all day long. The noise gets so loud that sometimes it's hard to hear God amidst it all. Don't be afraid to find a quiet place so you can speak and listen to the Savior.

Let go of all the voices that are constantly barking at you, and let God's voice be a soothing balm to your soul.

I say this for your own benefit, not to lay any restraint upon you, but to promote good order and to secure your undivided devotion to the Lord.

—1 Corinthians 7:35 (ESV)

Hoping for a Child

THERE ARE MANY REASONS a woman may find herself unable to conceive. For those who want to have a child, the pain can be almost unbearable. If you struggle with infertility, know you are not alone. Sarai, the wife of Abram, couldn't conceive until she was 90. Hannah was thought to be crazy when the priests heard her quietly mumbling prayers to God, wishing and hoping for a child. Even Rachel, the beloved wife of Jacob, didn't conceive for many years, but God still blessed them. For those who don't or can't conceive, maybe God already has a child in mind for you, whether through adoption or mentoring.

Let go of the worry that comes with infertility, and let God bless you in a multitude of ways.

He gives the barren woman a home, making her the joyous mother of children. Praise the LORD!

—PSALM 113:9 (ESV)

Seeking Balance

YOU KNOW THOSE PEOPLE. They climb ladders at work, keep a perfect house, have happy marriages and children who maintain honor roll while participating in extracurricular activities. In your mind, these folks are overachievers. They see everything as an opportunity to conquer, while you struggle to keep up. But you aren't them and they aren't you. God didn't create us to be the same. All of our circumstances are not the same. Experiment with your time to see if you can balance your work and family life have-to-dos with your spiritual life and your God-wants-you-to-dos.

Let go of comparing yourself to overachievers, and let God bring a natural balance to your life.

But let each one test his own work, and then his reason to boast will be in himself alone and not in his neighbor.

—GALATIANS 6:4 (ESV)

Light of the World

THE BIBLE TELLS US that hell is utter and eternal darkness. If you've toured a cavern, you may have experienced what felt like utter darkness when a guide turned the lights off. But even that darkness doesn't compare to eternal darkness. On the other hand is light. In heaven there will be no need for lamps or even the sun, moon, and stars. The Light of the world and His radiance will be enough. Just as the moon and stars reflect the sun's light, we believers can bring light to a dark world by reflecting God's light.

Let go of hiding from the darkness; run to it, and let God's light shine through you.

The light shines in the darkness, and
the darkness has not overcome it.
—JOHN 1:5 (ESV)

New Directions

WE ALL GO THROUGH hard times in life. Unfortunately, some of us get stuck there and can't seem to work our way out. We keep walking the same road, making the same mistakes. We go through the same motions, expecting different results. You won't see change that way. Change requires a step in the opposite direction than you've already been going. As scary as it may be, change is often good for us, and if we are in the will of God, He will be there each step of the way. We won't need to walk alone. Change starts by taking one step.

Let go of your fear of change; instead, embrace it, and let God guide you in making your life better.

The heart of man plans his way, but the LORD establishes his steps.

—PROVERBS 16:9 (ESV)

Positive Change

HAVE YOU EVER HEARD of paying it forward? The idea is that instead of paying someone back for something they did for you, you pass the good deed along to a new person. It doesn't matter if the person you're "paying" deserves it or not. We don't deserve Christ's love for us, but He took our punishment anyway. He is the ultimate example of paying it forward. Make today a day of changes, whether big or small. Do something for someone else that will positively impact his day or even change his life.

Let go of thinking you need to pay people back; instead, let God show you someone who needs you today.

*And as you wish that others would
do to you, do so to them.*
—LUKE 6:31 (ESV)

Power in Perspective

KNOW SOMEONE WHO HATES her job? Often, all the person can think about is how much she doesn't want to go to work every day. But what if you could encourage her to change perspective long enough to get through this season of her life? Encourage her to look at the big picture and set goals—perhaps a new job down the road. We can't always change the situation we're in immediately, or sometimes at all, but we can look at it from a different angle, gaining a new perspective and outlook on life.

Let go of the negative views, and let God help you see from a positive perspective.

An intelligent heart acquires knowledge, and the ear of the wise seeks knowledge.

—PROVERBS 18:15 (ESV)

Broken Hearts, Clean Hearts

THERE WILL BE DAYS when we fall out of fellowship with God. Unfortunately, when that happens, He must often resort to drastic measures. Our hearts need breaking. Why would a loving God ever want us to have broken hearts? He breaks our hearts to help us turn back to Him. Then He can give us a new, clean heart. Admitting our sin is a liberating feeling, especially once God restores joy to our lives. Broken hearts can be healed. God is just waiting for you to come to Him, broken, bruised, and repentant.

Let go of your broken heart, and let God put all the pieces of your life back together.

Create in me a clean heart, O God, and
renew a right spirit within me.
—PSALM 51:10 (ESV)

Collecting Tears

WE ALL HAVE loved ones with whom we cry from time to time. We also cry by and for ourselves. Sometimes we feel God doesn't know, see, or care about us, but that couldn't be further from the truth. Take comfort in knowing God does care deeply. God sings to us: "The LORD your God is in your midst, a mighty one who will save; he will rejoice over you with gladness; he will quiet you by his love; he will exult over you with loud singing" (Zephaniah 3:17 ESV). He collects our tears in a bottle. Only Someone who loves deeply would do that.

Let go of your sadness, and let God sing His love song to you.

You have kept count of my tossings; put my tears in your bottle. Are they not in your book?

—PSALM 56:8 (ESV)

Preparing to Worship

DOES YOUR SUNDAY morning involve fighting among the kids? Lost shoes? Lost keys? Scrambling around? By the time you get to church, you're exhausted and not in a state of worship. Before the Israelites went to the temple, they spent three days preparing themselves. Life gets busy and our worship often suffers. Before Sunday, prepare yourself. Make sure your family has everything ready. Prepare your heart and mind by spending time in prayer. Ask God to open you up to hear the message He has for you during the worship service. Ask that your worship draw you closer to Him.

Let go of the hustle and bustle of Sunday mornings, and let God prepare you ahead of time for worship.

It is good to give thanks to the LORD, to sing praises to your name, O Most High.
—PSALM 92:1 (ESV)

Holding a Grudge

PEOPLE ARE SO SENSITIVE today. Someone makes an offhand comment and another person takes offense and has hurt feelings. Not only do we hang on to those feelings, but we plot to get even, get revenge. Sometimes we just need to let things go. If there really is an issue, if someone really did hurt you, you might need to go to that person and talk about it. Maybe she didn't mean it. Many disagreements start over a simple misunderstanding. If someone has hurt you, go to her today if at all possible. Don't let the hurt fester.

Let go of revenge, and let God guide your words as you attempt to fix a relationship.

So also my heavenly father will do to every one of you,
if you do not forgive your brother from your heart.

—Matthew 18:35 (ESV)

Worship Is Action

PSALM 100 is all about worship. It's a wonderful guide for us when it comes to our own worship. If you read through the short Psalm, you'll notice something. This chapter is full of action verbs. The NIV uses "shout," "worship," "come," "know," "enter," "give thanks," and "praise." Do you know what that suggests? Our worship must be active. We can't just do nothing. The Bible tells us that "faith without works is dead" (James 2:20). We can't worship without action, and we can't have faith without action.

Let go of any laziness you may have when it comes to worship, and let God help you create a list of actionable ways to worship Him.

You see that faith was active along with his works,
and faith was completed by his works.

—JAMES 2:22 (ESV)

Pearl of Great Price

THERE'S A SAYING, "The value of a lost item is determined by the seeker." How often do we lose our keys? Forget where we parked? Misplace that report for work or school? In those moments, the lost item becomes pretty important. We search high and low, willing to give just about anything to find what we've lost and desperately need. That's what Christ does for us. He seeks us out and draws us to Himself. We are the pearl of great price mentioned in Matthew 13. God put such great value on each of us that He sent His son to die on the cross. You are a pearl of the greatest price!

Let go of feelings of low self-esteem, and let God prove how valuable you are to Him.

For the Son of Man came to seek and to save the lost.
—LUKE 19:10 (ESV)

Who Are You Becoming?

"SHE MUST BE his daughter. Look at her eyes." Whose eyes do you have—do they resemble a parent's, a grandparent's, maybe an aunt's or uncle's? In the Christian life we need to strive to become more like Christ. While you might have your father's eyes, we as believers need to have our Father's eyes. We need to endeavor to walk like Him, to talk like Him, and to act like Him.

Let go of the ways of the world, and let God nurture you to become more and more like Him every day.

Whoever says he abides in him ought to walk in the same way in which he walked.

—1 John 2:6 (ESV)

Ambassadors for Christ

THE DEFINITION of an ambassador is someone who represents the policies and interests of a country or organization. An ambassador has the plans and best interests of the company or organization for whom she works in mind. As ambassadors for Christ, it is our duty to live out the plans Christ has for us. We need to share His love so others can learn of Him and accept Him as Savior. Christ's plans will make our lives and the lives of those with whom we come in contact better. When we truly live for God, His plans will become our plans as we grow to be more in tune with Him.

Let go of your plans, and let God's plans be evident in your life.

Therefore, we are ambassadors for Christ, God making his appeal through us. We implore you on behalf of Christ, be reconciled to God.

—2 CORINTHIANS 5:20 (ESV)

Secure in God

A WOMAN DEALT with severe insecurities that began when her father left her family for another woman. After that, her father was very rarely in her life. Her insecurities followed her into her own marriage. Her husband couldn't even accidentally glance in the direction of another woman. She accused her husband of cheating, even when there was no real evidence. Many situations in life might cause us to be insecure. Wherever that insecurity comes from, the solution is the same. Only through Christ will we find security.

Let go of any insecurities you may have, and let God be all the refuge you need.

There is no fear in love, but perfect love casts out fear.
For fear has to do with punishment, and whoever
fears has not been perfected in love.

—1 JOHN 4:18 (ESV)

Dual Citizenship

MANY PEOPLE ENJOY the benefits of dual citizenship. They can vote, work, own property, and take advantage of educational benefits. But there is one major drawback: usually, only one country has the citizen's loyalty and heart. In the Christian life, there is no such thing as dual citizenship. You are either a citizen of heaven or you're not. You can't be loyal to both God and the world. The Bible tells us in Matthew 6:24 that "no one can serve two masters." Today, you need to choose where your loyalty lies.

Let go of whatever pulls you to be a citizen of this world, and let God hold your loyalty.

But our citizenship is in heaven, and from it we await a savior, the Lord Jesus Christ.

—PHILIPPIANS 3:20 (ESV)

Precious Creation

DO YOU EVER FEEL completely unloved and unappreciated? Most of us do at some point. Sometimes we feel we will never get out of that funk. Know that God loves you as a most precious creation. Read though the creation story in Genesis 1–2. God created all sorts of wonderful things, *everything*. But when it came to us, we were the only creation into which God breathed the breath of life. God loved us so much, He gave us His breath. That should make you feel truly loved.

Let go of your feeling of being unloved, and let God wrap His arms of love around you.

Then the LORD God formed the man of dust from the ground and breathed into his nostrils the breath of life, and the man became a living creature.

—GENESIS 2:7 (ESV)

Praying Together

THERE IS NOT A WHOLE LOT that feels better than knowing you are united in prayer with like-minded people. You don't need to be all together or even praying at exactly the same time. Daniel knew the benefits of asking godly friends to pray for him. When we are at a crisis point, we need to ask our friends to pray. Giving all the details isn't necessary. When we do this, we are putting our hope in God.

Let go of panic when stressful situations arise; instead, ask trusted friends to pray, and let God give an answer.

Then Daniel went to his house and made the matter known to Hananiah, Mishael, and Azariah, his companions, and told them to seek mercy from the God of heaven concerning this mystery.

—DANIEL 2:17–18A (ESV)

Using Time Wisely

EVEN IF WE'RE USUALLY good managers of our time, days come when we can't seem to complete anything. We flit from one project to another, never finishing. At the end of the day, we're exhausted with nothing to show for it. The day has been a waste. The Bible tells us there's a time for everything; however, wasting time isn't on the list. God gave us twenty-four hours each day to use as we see fit. Maybe we should start thinking about how God would have us use our time.

Let go of wasting away the day, and let God show you how to use each minute wisely.

Give her of the fruit of her hands, and let
her works praise her in the gates.
—PROVERBS 31:13 (ESV)

Arguing with Fools

HAVE YOU EVER KNOWN someone who liked to argue about everything? It didn't matter what you said or how much knowledge you had; she knew more and set out to debate everything. What are we to do? Ecclesiastes 3:7b tells us there is a time to "keep silence, and a time to speak." It's much wiser not to answer and play into the hands of a fool, especially if that person is only looking to tear you down. A fool's mind is often closed in an argument, and when you argue back, you're just as foolish.

Let go of stooping to the level of fools, and let God win arguments for you.

Answer not a fool according to his folly, lest you be like him yourself. Answer a fool according to his folly, lest he be wise in his own eyes.

—Proverbs 26:4-5 (ESV)

Jehovah Shalom

THERE ISN'T MUCH PEACE in the world these days with countries and families constantly at war. Life around us can be chaos, but sometimes we need to find a moment of peace amid that chaos. Sometimes we need a quiet place of rest. When we have a relationship with God, peace is always at our fingertips. He is Jehovah-Shalom ("Jehovah Send Peace"). No matter what we are facing today, peace for our hearts is just a prayer away. The only place we can find peace is in the presence of God. If you have accepted Him as your Savior, hallelujah, you are always in the presence of God!

Let go of the noise and chaos of the world, and let God be your Jehovah Shalom.

And the peace of God, which surpasses all understanding, will guard your hearts and your minds in Christ Jesus.
—PHILIPPIANS 4:7 (ESV)

Peace in a Shadow

DID YOU EVER PLAY with your shadow as a child? Depending on the position of the sun, the shadow was either short and squat or tall and thin. Maybe you tried to catch up to or run away from your shadow. But neither ever happened. Your shadow and you always met up and connected right at the feet. There's a Shadow who can bring us comfort. It's God. We can rest in His shadow when all is well or take refuge there when storms of life are blowing and raging around us. During those times God truly is our refuge and strength.

Let go of trying to hide in your own shadow, and let God's shadow be where you find peace.

Have mercy on me, my God, have mercy on me, for in you I take refuge. I will take refuge in the shadow of your wings until the disaster has passed.

—Psalm 57:1 (NIV)

Making Plans

SOME OF US are serious planners; spontaneity isn't in our blood. Regardless of our planning, not everything works out as we hope. There are the times when God's plans for us aren't the ones we have for ourselves. Maybe you thought you would live in the country but wound up in the city. Perhaps you were planning to have two kids but had three. In all of those instances, God knew best. You were right within His plans.

Let go of planning every detail of your life, and let God direct your paths.

Declare what is to be, present it—let them take counsel together. Who foretold this long ago, who declared it from the distant past? Was it not I, the LORD? And there is no God apart from me, a righteous God and a Savior; there is none but me.

—ISAIAH 45:21 (NIV)

Shining for God

A SIMPLE SMILE can be so uplifting. Some people just make us smile. When your loved one smiles at you from across a crowded room, with a smile reserved just for you, you can't help but smile back. Maybe a phone call from a child or parent can make you smile. When God thinks of you, He smiles. You are one of His precious children whom He loves more than you will ever realize. He constantly has us on His mind. He must smile a lot!

Let go of your grumpy face, give someone a smile, and let God have one more reason to shine His smile down on you.

The LORD delights in those who fear him, who put their hope in his unfailing love.

—PSALM 147:11 (NIV)

The Blessing of Church

SOMEONE ONCE SAID, "Going to church doesn't make me a better Christian." Church attendance is not a requirement for a believer, but you're missing out if you don't go. You might learn a lot through TV church, but one critical component is missing: fellowship. Godly friends make us better Christians. Proverbs 27:17 tells us that "Iron sharpens iron." We need that.

Let go of thinking you don't need the fellowship of other godly people, and let God bring true, Christian friends into your life through church.

Not neglecting to meet together, as is the habit of some, but encouraging one another, and all the more as you see the Day drawing near.

—HEBREWS 10:25 (ESV)

No Questions Asked

MARY, JESUS' MOTHER, is a heroine. Surprised at night by an angelic visitor telling her she was with child, she pretty much responded with, "OK." Wouldn't you have been panicking? Wouldn't you have been asking all kinds of questions and wondering what people would think? But Mary heard a word from God and she accepted it, no questions and no arguing. When God puts us on a path we had no intention of walking down, how do we respond?

Let go of arguing with the Lord and His plans for you, and let God draw you into a more fulfilling life as you obey.

And Mary said, "Behold, I am the servant of the Lord;
let it be to me according to your word."
And the angel departed from her.
—LUKE 1:38 (ESV)

Tolerance of Sin

OVER THE LAST couple of decades, people's views of sin have definitely changed. If someone had done something bad in private, he hoped to keep it a secret. But what was once guarded in private is now flaunted out in the open without a care who sees, because society has become tolerant of sin. God knows our secrets, and it breaks His heart when we do sin. Just because the world sins and thinks nothing of it certainly doesn't mean we should act the same.

Let go of any tolerance of sin you might have, and let God open your eyes to see what is sin in His eyes.

He who justifies the wicked and he who condemns the righteous are both alike an abomination to the LORD.
—PROVERBS 17:15 (ESV)

Who Is God?

WHO IS GOD? Your answer to that question will say more about you than it does about God. Some people have called him a prophet or a good man. Others call him the promised Messiah who offers hope, peace, and light. Those who have had to completely put their faith and trust in God and those who study the Word daily know Him on a much deeper and more personal level. We can't put God in a box. Who God is might be as different for each of us as our experiences have been with Him.

Let go of believing you can't learn more about Him, and let God reveal Himself as you delve into the Scriptures and see Him in your life.

The next day he saw Jesus coming toward him, and said, "Behold, the Lamb of God, who takes away the sin of the world!"
—JOHN 1:29 (ESV)

What to Do

IF YOU READ the account of Jesus in the Garden of Gethsemane, you'll notice that the disciples are with Jesus, but they don't seem to know what to do. They probably prayed some, but the truth is there wasn't much they could do. Jesus had to do it on His own. Gethsemane means "mill" or "winepress." This name is symbolic of Christ's being crushed to extract something we desperately needed from Him—salvation. Sometimes when a friend is going through a difficult time, there's nothing we can do except pray. That may not seem like much, but it's the best we can do.

Let go of the need to fix everything for others, and let God be the One to help them persevere.

Then he said to them, "My soul is overwhelmed
with sorrow to the point of death.
Stay here and keep watch with me."
—Matthew 26:38 (ESV)

God of Miracles

THE GOSPELS ARE FULL of miracles that Jesus performed. It's baffling that people who witnessed these miracles still chose not to believe. Jesus may not be physically here on earth anymore, but that doesn't mean miracles no longer happen. There are medical mysteries that can only be attributed to the healing hand of God. Financial blessings have occurred that can only be counted as miracles. Yet even people who witness miracles today still choose not to believe. What do you believe?

Let go of your unbelief, and let God prove He is still a God of miracles.

Jesus performed many other signs in the presence of his disciples, which are not recorded in this book. But these are written that you may believe that Jesus is the Messiah, the Son of God, and that by believing you may have life in his name.

—JOHN 20:30-31 (NIV)

Jumping for the Lord

CHILDREN LOVE TO JUMP—on beds, over puddles, anytime they're given an opportunity. The Bible tells us of a man who jumped. He didn't necessarily jump for fun, but simply because he could. Through Christ's power, Peter and John helped the man stand. He didn't just stand; he jumped—and he continued jumping as he followed them into the Temple. Do you jump because you're excited about what God is doing in your life? In spite of how silly we may look, maybe it's time we started. At least we'll draw an audience with whom we could share our stories.

Let go of your inhibitions, and let God be glorified when you jump for Him.

He jumped to his feet and began to walk. Then he went with them into the temple courts, walking and jumping, and praising God.
—ACTS 3:8 (NIV)

Bondage versus Freedom

WHEN PAUL WROTE Galatians, he was writing mostly to slaves. There were millions of slaves in the Roman Empire who desired to be free. Although they couldn't be free from their masters, Paul shared that they could be free in Christ. We too can enjoy freedom in Christ. While we may not be in slavery, we can still be in bondage to our jobs, our families, and any of the situations in which we might find ourselves.

Let go of your chains, and let God provide the freedom you so desire.

It is for freedom that Christ has set us free.
Stand firm, then, and do not let yourselves be
burdened again by a yoke of slavery.
—GALATIANS 5:1 (NIV)

Godspeed

EVER HEAR THE EXPRESSION "Godspeed"? The meaning is, "God go with you." Another definition is, "the wish of success of one beginning a journey." We are all on a journey—the journey of life. It's a spiritual journey on which God does go with us each day. We travel different roads with experiences all our own, but God is with each of us all along the way. Whatever road you find yourself on, make sure you go with God. He is waiting for you. He wants to walk along with you. Take comfort and know that you are never alone. You go with God. Godspeed.

Let go of trying to navigate this life by yourself, and let God walk alongside you.

Therefore, as you received Christ Jesus the Lord, so walk in him.

—COLOSSIANS 2:6 (ESV)

The Best Is Yet to Come

JESUS' FIRST MIRACLE was at a wedding, where the hosts ran out of wine. This turn of events would have been an utter embarrassment in Bible times. So Jesus' mother urged Him to step in. He took water and turned it into wine. In our lives, we face trials. At the end of our lives, the experiences we had in life, whether good or bad, will fade away. For all of us who have accepted Christ as Savior, He is saving the best for last. Look at all He has already brought you through. Look at all the wonderful things He has accomplished through you. The best is yet to come: heaven.

Let go of dwelling on your past, and let God show you what you have in store in His house.

And said to him, "Everyone serves the good wine first, and when people have drunk freely, then the poor wine. But you have kept the good wine until now."

—JOHN 2:10 (ESV)

Bloom and Grow

IT'S ENJOYABLE TO DRIVE through the countryside and see a field full of blooming wildflowers. Flowers don't care where they are planted; they bloom and grow wherever a seed has landed and sprouted. We could all learn a lesson from wildflowers. There will come a time in our lives when we may not be happy with where we are, physically, mentally, or spiritually. But just like those wildflowers, we need to bloom and grow where God has planted us. We may only be there temporarily, so we need to make the best use of that time.

Let go of complaining about your present location, and let God nurture you into a beautiful flower for His purpose.

But grow in the grace and knowledge of our Lord and Savior Jesus Christ. To him be the glory both now and to the day of eternity. Amen.

—2 Peter 3:18 (ESV)

Marriage Mending

DIVORCE IS SO EASY and common. The traditional family—one father, one mother, and their children—is not the norm anymore, even among Christians. Even if your marriage is far from perfect, if there has been no infidelity or abuse of any kind, remember that you made a commitment to God on your wedding day. Make time to pray for your spouse. Pray with your spouse, if possible. Seek counseling, if necessary, that will help you both put God first.

Let go of taking the easy way out of a marriage, and let God heal and grow your relationship.

So they are no longer two but one flesh. What therefore God has joined together, let not man separate.

—MATTHEW 19:6 (ESV)

When Kids Turn Away

A WOMAN WAS ASKED if she felt like a failure as a mom because one of her sons had made a string of bad decisions. She responded, "My husband and I had him in church every time the doors were open. We taught him about God at home. He knows the truth. The decisions he made were his own." Some of our children will turn away from God. Our kids will make mistakes. It's true that some of the decisions we made will affect them, but they are responsible for their own actions.

Let go of any guilt you carry because of your children's choices, and let God be their Judge.

There is a way that seems right to a man, but its end is the way to death.

—PROVERBS 14:12 (ESV)

Root Systems

TREES ARE AMAZING creations. When standing near a tree, we often feel awe when we look up; however, what we don't see is just as awesome. The root system of a tree is twice as big as the crown. That root system supports and draws nourishment for the tree. As Christians we also need a good root system. It starts with our own study of the Bible, our family, our church, our friends, and prayer. We need all of these things to help us grow stronger in the Lord and know how God would have us live our lives.

Let go of any shallow roots, and let God provide what you need to deepen your roots.

He is like a tree planted by streams of water that yields its fruit in its season, and its leaf does not wither. In all that he does, he prospers.

—PSALM 1:3 (ESV)

Cereal for Dinner

SOME DAYS START out crazy. Some days become worse when monkey wrenches are thrown in. There's car trouble when you have errands to run. A sick child just before the recital. The lunch you managed to dump down the front of your shirt while trying to cram some food down your throat as you speed to the most important meeting of your career. Those are frequently the days we end up serving cold cereal for dinner. Those are the days we're down on ourselves for not being able to do it all. We don't need to be superheroes every day.

Let go of thinking you need to do it all every day, and let God remind you that His mercies are new every morning.

Whatever your hand finds to do, do it with your might.
—ECCLESIASTES 9:10A (ESV)

Prepared the Way

AT LEAST OCCASIONALLY, we don't understand what God is telling us to do. But we don't always need to understand; we need to obey. That's the way it should be when God gives direction. We must go, having faith that God has already gone ahead and prepared the way. Knowing God has gone ahead gives us strength and confidence to take the steps as God directs. The next time you feel God giving you direction, take some time to pray and make sure it's His voice you hear and not anyone else's. Then be confident as you walk toward that goal, knowing He has gone before you.

Let go of worries about what He is telling you to do, and let God give direction at each step.

And your ears shall hear a word behind you, saying,
"This is the way, walk in it," when you turn to the
right or when you turn to the left.

—Isaiah 30:21 (ESV)

An Ear to Listen

WHEN YOU COME TOGETHER with friends and family, are you a talker or listener? Being the talker is fine once in a while, but we need to spend more time listening, and really listening, not just pretending to listen to appease someone. When we listen, we let others know that what they say is important. It might be a good idea to take note of how much you talk. If you talk more than you listen, you may need to make some changes.

Let go of carrying conversations by yourself, and let God remind you to use your ears more than your mouth.

Know this, my beloved brothers: let every person be quick to hear, slow to speak, slow to anger.

—JAMES 1:19 (ESV)

Giving Up Life

THROUGHOUT HISTORY people have given their lives to save others. Many of us would do that for a family member. But what about giving your life for a stranger? Probably not many would do that. How many people would give up their life for you? But two thousand years ago, Someone did give up His life for us. Apparently, we weren't even worthy to take on our own punishment. Because Jesus loved us so much, He gave His life for ours. Ask that question again: Who would give up their life for me? Someone already did.

Let go of believing you aren't important to anyone, and let God remind you that He gave up His one and only begotten Son for you.

Greater love has no one than this, that someone lay down his life for his friends.

—JOHN 15:13 (ESV)

But. . .

READING THROUGH THE PSALMS of David, we can see the ups and downs of his spiritual life. Our spiritual lives often follow that same roller coaster. Some days we shout from the mountaintops; other days we're in the depths of despair. In spite of David's low points, he still looked to God. David often uses the word *but*. *But* seems insignificant; however, David uses it realizing he is out of his own strength and must turn to God for His. We, too, run out of strength. When this happens, remember *but*: where human strength ends, God's strength begins.

Let go of doing everything by your own strength, and let God be the strength you need.

They confronted me in the day of my calamity,
but the LORD was my support.
—PSALM 18:18 (ESV)

Leveling Up

LIFE IS FULL OF LEVELS. Buildings have levels. There are different levels of security. We are always striving to reach the next level, to move up a step. Then there's God. How often do we try to bring Him down to our level? God is unchanging. He is the same always. We need to move closer to Him. We'll never be on the same level as God, but that's what makes Him God. It's striving to be like Him that makes us grow in our faith and grow closer to Him.

Let go of trying to bring Him down to your level, and let God's level be the goal for which you reach.

For I the LORD do not change.

—MALACHI 3:6A (ESV)

Believe, Live, Love

LIVING A LIFE OF PERFECTION is a lofty goal we'll never reach. If we know it's impossible, why don't we just live however we please? God wants us as believers to recognize our need for Him. God wants us to come to Him, imperfections and all. All He asks is that we believe. Once we do that, everything else will fall into place. When we believe in Him, we want to know more about Him. As we learn more about Him, we begin to understand how we should live. Then we will want to reach toward the lofty goal of perfection in His love.

Let go of the idea of becoming a perfect human being, and let God give you understanding of what it means to try to live as He did.

Those who are in the flesh cannot please God.
—ROMANS 8:8 (ESV)

Simple Living

TODAY THERE IS SO MUCH coming at us all the time. It's a relief to go "off the grid" for a while with no TV, Internet, or phone. We don't need up-to-the-minute depressing news. We don't need to know what everyone ate for lunch. That overload is exactly what Paul was talking about. He encouraged the Thessalonians not to worry about what everyone else was doing. Go off the grid for a while. Read a book. Play games with your family. You may not want to go back.

Let go of the constant chatter, and let God show you how simple and quiet is better.

And to aspire to live quietly, and to mind your own affairs, and to work with your hands, as we instructed you.

—1 THESSALONIANS 4:11 (ESV)

Uncovering Idols

IF SOMEONE WERE TO ASK if you had any idols your life, you would probably cover your mouth in shock. If you objectively examined your life, you might feel the need to cover your mouth in shock again when you realize you do have idols. Not all idols are made of gold and silver. An idol is anything that steals time away from God. Our lives are busy and filled with tasks for taking care of ourselves and our families, but it's when those to-dos get out of control that they become idols.

Let go of any extra activities that take away time from prayer and Bible study, and let God permanently remove those idols for you.

You shall have no other gods before me.

—EXODUS 20:3 (ESV)

Eternal Remedy

PAIN COMES IN MANY FORMS. It can be physical, mental, or emotional. No matter what kind of pain you have today, there is one remedy for all. God can take away all the hurts, but that relief might not come in the way we think it should. God may not take away our physical illness, and the pain from losing someone you love doesn't dissipate overnight. God may not take all our pain away completely, but with His power we can overcome it. He will give us strength to persevere and get out of bed each morning.

Let go of any pain you're holding on to, and let God be the strength you need to survive.

When you pass through the waters, I will be with you; and through the rivers, they shall not overwhelm you; when you walk through fire you shall not be burned, and the flame shall not consume you.

—ISAIAH 43:2 (ESV)

God's Messengers

HAVE YOU EVER RECEIVED an answer to prayer in a puzzling form? Maybe it was a phone call from a stranger, a letter from a friend, verses posted on social media, or even a conversation. Don't underestimate these messengers from God. God will use whom he pleases to make His will known to you. God influences hearts that communicate His Word, love, and grace to you. Once you receive your answer, it's your turn to step out in faith.

Let go of ignoring answers from seemingly impossible sources, and let God speak to you through one of His messengers.

For he will command his angels concerning you to guard you in all your ways.

—Psalm 91:11 (ESV)

Heaven in a Hug

SOMETHING SPECIAL HAPPENS when a small child wraps her arms around you and squeezes with affection. Suddenly, sadness or that bad day can melt away. Think about what a hug from a friend can do. It can offer support, reassurance, love, and sympathy, all without a word being said. Open your eyes to see who around you simply needs a hug. God sends comfort to those who need it, and we can be the vessel He chooses if we make ourselves aware.

Let go of your standoffish tendencies, and let God give comfort through your arms.

Praise be to the God and Father of our Lord Jesus Christ, the Father of compassion and the God of all comfort, who comforts us in all our troubles, so that we can comfort those in any trouble with the comfort we ourselves receive from God.

—2 Corinthians 1:3–4 (NIV)

Writing Your Funeral

A COMMON SCHOOL ASSIGNMENT is to write your own epitaph or funeral. It forces us to think about the future and the meaning of our lives. So where do we start? It doesn't matter how many people we know; it's how we touch them while we're alive that writes our epitaph. What have you done that makes a difference to others? Will anyone miss you when you're gone? Go to God and ask if you have been following where and to whom He leads.

Let go of life being all about you, and let God show you how to touch the lives of others.

You make known to me the path of life; in your presence there is fullness of joy; at your right hand are pleasures forevermore.

—PSALM 16:11 (ESV)

A Glimpse of Heaven

WE'RE OFTEN TOLD to focus on and live in the moment—not to jump ahead of ourselves too much. Or we get wrapped up in the future and our successful place in it, only as measured by the world's standard. But do you ever think about what heaven is like? There's nothing wrong with looking to the future if we have our eyes set on our eternal heavenly home rather than on our temporary earthly one.

Let go of thinking that heaven is far into the future, and let God show your heart a little glimpse of Paradise today.

...rejoice that your names are written in heaven.
—LUKE 10:20B (ESV)

Just the Beginning

SOME PEOPLE THINK if they accept Christ as their Savior, that's it—that's all they need do. They don't want to go to hell, and salvation is their free ticket to heaven. But they're wrong. Salvation is just the beginning, the beginning of a new way of life. If you have sincerely accepted Christ, you will want to change. God expects more from us than just sitting around. We need to give God our all and further His kingdom while we await His return. We need to share the Good News that we have already believed and encourage others to accept it as well.

Let go of waiting, and let God point out ways you could be working in the meantime.

Thus you will recognize them by their fruits.

—MATTHEW 7:20 (ESV)

God's Grace

GRACE IS SOMETHING we often need to work hard at extending to people. If people suffer consequences for their actions, we may feel no sympathy. That attitude does not come from God. He is the epitome of grace. If it were not for God's grace, we would be destined to live an eternity in hell. None of us can earn God's grace. It's a gift He freely gives. If God had enough grace to make us one of His children, we should emulate and freely give that grace to the people with whom we come in contact.

Let go of all the times you want to lash out at others, and let God extend His grace to them through you.

In him we have redemption through his blood, the forgiveness of our trespasses, according to the riches of his grace.

—EPHESIANS 1:7 (ESV)

Sharing Wisdom

WE KNOW WE HAVE different talents, but did you know you can use those as doors to share God's love? Sharing what we know can be a way of meeting people. You can share a love of scrapbooking by offering classes. You can share a love of painting by teaching others. Through these opportunities, you may find you are also able to share your testimonies. Do you have a talent others would enjoy knowing more about? Set up classes, encourage people to bring friends, and share what God has done in your life.

Let go of believing you have nothing to share, and let God's story shine as you share your talents.

From everyone who has been given much, much will be demanded; and from the one who has been entrusted with much, much more will be asked.
—LUKE 12:48B (NIV)

Not Sorry

PARENTS SOMETIMES FORCE children to apologize when they really aren't sorry. Kids may say the words, but with no remorse behind them. They may be sorry they were caught, but not sorry for their actions. Children aren't the only ones who offer empty apologies. In Matthew 27, Judas was only sorry after he realized what the consequences were for his actions. He went to the priests who had paid him and tried to make things right, but it was too late for Judas. It may not be too late for you, though. Think before you act so you won't need to be sorry for anything.

Let go of actions or words that might be hurtful to someone, and let God show you any areas where you do need to be sorry.

Therefore confess your sins to each other and pray for each other so that you may be healed.

—JAMES 5:16A (NIV)

God's Way, Not Our Way

AS HUMANS, we can be manipulative. We know exactly what to say and do to get our own way. Manipulation isn't a new tactic. When King Herod was celebrating his birthday with his wife, who was also his sister-in-law, she schooled her daughter in manipulation. After the girl danced for Herod and his officials, he was so pleased he offered her anything she wanted. With her mother's influence, she chose the head of John the Baptist on a platter. John the Baptist died that day. While that example may be an extreme case, we do need to be careful we don't manipulate others. When we do, our true colors come out, and they aren't pretty.

Let go of manipulating, and let God be the Ruler of your life and the lives of others.

You shall not wrong one another, but you shall fear your God, for I am the LORD your God.

—LEVITICUS 25:17 (ESV)

Spiritual Weapons

WE ARE GIVEN the armor of God in Ephesians 6. Our armor includes the belt of truth, breastplate of righteousness, Gospel of peace, shield of faith, and helmet of salvation. These items are all protective, but we do have one defensive weapon as well—the Sword of the Spirit. The Bible is our only defense against evil. How well can you wield your sword?

Let go of always being on the offensive, and let God's word help you defend the faith.

For the weapons of our warfare are not of the flesh but have divine power to destroy strongholds.
—2 CORINTHIANS 10:4 (ESV)

Reverence and Awe

REVERENCE AND *AWE* should be words we think of when it comes to worshiping God. But so often we flippantly come before God, whether in a church for corporate worship or at home in private prayer. Many see God as a genie who will grant every wish, but He's not. We need to come before Him with reverent hearts and in awe of who He is. He deserves our respect just for who He is. When we give Him the reverence and awe He is worthy of, our lives get changed in the process.

Let go of any flippancy you may have in your worship, and let God be praised sincerely.

Therefore let us be grateful for receiving a kingdom that cannot be shaken, and thus let us offer to God acceptable worship, with reverence and awe.

—Hebrews 12:28 (ESV)

Family Legacy

MORE THAN ONE HEROD is mentioned in the Bible. Herod the Great, Herod Antipas, and Herod Agrippa I were three generations of kings, one just as evil as the other. Herod the Great ordered all baby boys killed, hoping to eliminate baby Jesus. Herod Antipas killed John the Baptist. Herod Agrippa I killed James, one of Jesus' disciples, and attempted to kill Peter. This was quite the family legacy. What is the legacy you are leaving to your children? Is it one of faith in God? Observe your children to see their actions and what type of legacy you are leaving.

Let go of anything that might be a negative legacy, and let God give you wisdom that you can pass on to the next generation.

We will not hide them from their children, but tell to the coming generation the glorious deeds of the LORD, and his might, and the wonders that he has done.

—PSALM 78:4 (ESV)

A Quiet Place

FROM THE AGE OF THIRTY to thirty-three, Jesus spent all of His time ministering to others. In the short span between that ministry and His death, He needed some peace and quiet. So he spent much-needed time with His closest friends, the disciples, and just being. He needed to get away from the large crowds and minister privately to his disciples by washing their feet before eating the Passover meal. We, too, need to find a quiet place to spend time with our closest Christian friends. That time will help rejuvenate us when we're tired spiritually.

Let go of pretending you never need a moment's rest, and let God grant you peace and quiet.

And he said to them, "Come away by yourselves to a desolate place and rest a while."
—MARK 6:31A (ESV)

Elohim

"IN THE BEGINNING, God…" That God is Elohim. Elohim is the first name the Bible gives us for God. It means strength and power. Elohim is the covenant-keeping God of Abraham. His power created everything. He is the Creator who is mighty and strong. It's interesting to note that Elohim is actually plural, pointing to the Trinity. From the very beginning of the Bible, God's power is evident. Who else could speak an entire universe into existence?

Let go of thinking you're something on your own, and let God remind you He is your Creator.

In the beginning, God created the heavens and the earth.
—Genesis 1:1 (ESV)

Intercessory Prayer

HAVE YOU EVER PRAYED on behalf of someone else? Many biblical figures practiced intercessory prayer. Moses prayed on behalf of the Israelites, who just couldn't seem to obey God's commands. Job interceded for his children, who had some bad habits. If these two giants in the faith believed intercessory prayer was worthwhile, maybe we should as well. When we lament that *all* we can do is pray, take comfort that the *best* thing we can do is pray.

Let go of believing there is nothing you can do for others lost in sin, and let God take over when you place them at His feet.

So Moses returned to the LORD and said, "Alas, this people has sinned a great sin. They have made for themselves gods of gold. But now, if you will forgive their sin—but if not, please blot me out of your book that you have written."

—EXODUS 32:31–32 (ESV)

Revival of Hearts

BEFORE THE PROTESTANT Reformation, people of the church needed to depend on what leaders said when it came to the Bible. Commoners did not have their own copies. Unfortunately, those leaders were often wrong. Since the Bible was interpreted in the language of the people and printed at an affordable cost, people have been able to read it for themselves. That's when revival happened. When we look into God's Word for ourselves, that's when revival happens for us as well. Do you make a habit of delving into the Scriptures?

Let go of thinking you can't understand the Bible, and let God speak to your heart through its pages.

Will you not revive us again, that your people may rejoice in you?

—Psalm 85:6 (ESV)

Therefore

WHEN STUDYING THE BIBLE, it is important to study each word individually. Studying a book of the Bible as a whole is helpful as well as understanding a little bit about the culture of society at the time each book was written. One word you need to pay attention to is *therefore*. Theological wisdom says, "If you read *therefore*, you go back and see what it's there for." *Therefore* is a transition word; it lets you know that what you just read is about to be explained.

Let go of intimidation, and let God impress upon your heart what He says in His word.

Therefore, stay awake, for you do not know on what day your Lord is coming.
—MATTHEW 24:42 (ESV)

God Knew

IF WE COULD SEE the future, we might not befriend that person who will take advantage of us. We might change our diet if we had advance warning of health issues. We would step on the brake instead of the gas at that yellow light to avoid an accident. God is the only One who knows the future. He knew our future before it became our past. God knew before we were even born all the sinful acts we would commit, but He loved us anyway.

Let go of your past, and let God reveal your future with Him.

Peter said to him, "Lord, I am ready to go with you both to prison and to death." Jesus said, "I tell you, Peter, the rooster will not crow this day, until you deny three times that you know me."

—LUKE 22:33-34 (ESV)

El Shaddai

THERE'S A POWERFUL SONG entitled "El Shaddai" (He Is God Almighty). Listen to it when you're doubting or feeling lost. It will give you assurance that because our God is Almighty, we don't need to face our struggles alone. God is with us and He is much more capable of fighting our battles than we could ever dream of being. It doesn't matter if those battles are physical or spiritual; El Shaddai can conquer them all. It is only up to us to trust.

Let go of fighting battles on your own, and let God Almighty go before you.

By the God of your father who will help you, by the Almighty who will bless you with blessings of heaven above.
—GENESIS 49:25A (ESV)

Come Closer

WHEN A YOUNG GIRL first got glasses, she wasn't very good about keeping them clean. Her father would look at her strangely and then say, "Come closer." She obeyed, thinking there was something wrong. All of a sudden, he would lick his fingers and wipe them across her glasses. In her disgust at his slobber, she would go clean them. Eventually, she learned what he was trying to teach her. God begs us to come closer to Him so we can learn what His will is for our lives. The closer we are to God, the more restless we will be until we have accomplished what He has called us to do.

Let go of your tentativeness, and let God draw you closer.

Blessed is the one you choose and bring near,
to dwell in your courts!
—Psalm 65:4a (ESV)

Sharing Treasures

TEACHING IS ANOTHER WAY in which we can imitate Christ. But it doesn't require a traditional classroom setting. Think of teaching as simply sharing treasures with others. And what better treasures to share than Biblical gems of knowledge? When you learn something new, share it with excitement. After reading through the Bible so many times, one would think there is nothing more to learn. But then God opens His storehouse of knowledge and shows us something new.

Let go of hoarding your wisdom, and let God bless you through the gift of teaching.

Until I come, devote yourself to the public reading of Scripture, to exhortation, to teaching.
—1 TIMOTHY 4:13 (ESV)

Pointing to God

DEBORAH STANDS OUT as a woman of God in the Bible. She was a born leader and did her job well as one of the judges of Israel. She used her position to help others. She was an advisor, mediator, and counselor to whom others listened. One of Deborah's characteristics we can appreciate was that whenever someone praised her for doing a good job, she gave credit where credit was due: God. If you are in a position in which people look up to you, pray for God to give you wisdom. Point others to God wherever He has placed you.

Let go of thinking you have no influence, and let God use your position for good.

She used to sit under the palm of Deborah between Ramah and Bethel in the hill country of Ephraim, and the people of Israel came up to her for judgment.

—JUDGES 4:5 (ESV)

The Jealousy Trap

IF WE LOOK, there is always something to be jealous about. He has a better job. She doesn't need to work at all. Her husband is more understanding. His family lives nearby. Her mom is still alive. . . . We need to be thankful for what we have and where God has placed us. We may not always have everything we want, but have you ever thought maybe it's better that way? You can turn all of the above statements around. For example, he may have a better job, but how many hours does he work? Praise God for what you already have.

Let go of any jealousy, and let God bless you in unique ways.

A tranquil heart gives life to the flesh, but envy makes the bones rot.

—PROVERBS 14:30 (ESV)

The Veil

A BRIDE OFTEN WEARS a veil covering her face. The groom lifts that veil to see her radiant face. Moses also wore a veil over his radiant face. After spending time with God, his face shone so that no one could look at it. The veil both protected the Israelites and served as a form of judgment for their sinful ways. Moses removed the veil when talking to God, because God already saw him as he was. The same is true for us. God can see past any coverings we may use in an attempt to hide something; we have no secrets from Him.

Let go of trying to hide behind a veil, and let God see you as the child He already knows.

Whenever Moses went in before the Lord to speak with him, he would remove the veil, until he came out.

—Exodus 34:34a (ESV)

The Power of Salt

SALT AIDS in preservation. If you've ever cured ham or a slab of bacon, you know there is a lot of salt involved. In the Old Testament, the Israelites were commanded to use salt in their grain offerings. This command was to be a reminder of their covenant with God. Salt was a symbol of God's activity in their lives—and ours too. When we study God's Word, it penetrates, preserves, and heals our souls.

Let go of life with no flavor, and let God season it perfectly.

You shall season all your grain offerings with salt. You shall not let the salt of the covenant with your God be missing from your grain offering; with all your offerings you shall offer salt.

—LEVITICUS 2:13 (ESV)

Bread of Life

BREAD, IN SOME FORM or another, is a staple of almost every culture in the world. Bread can fill empty bellies and offer much-needed nourishment. While bread might satisfy our physical hunger for a time, we will need to eat again before long. When we accept Christ as our Savior, He becomes the Bread of our spiritual life. He is it. He is all we need. To maintain a relationship with Him, we must feed our souls. When we don't read the Bible and pray, we starve spiritually. Daily time spent with God will sustain us.

Let go of consuming what doesn't feed you spiritually, and let God be the Bread that gives you life.

I am the bread of life.

—JOHN 6:48 (ESV)

Make a Move

WE ALL STRUGGLE with laziness at times. But we can take it to God and pray each morning for productivity. God can help by nudging us to do "one more thing." We will never get *everything* done, but we can use time to the best of our ability. If you think you struggle with laziness, don't wait to bring the issue to God. If there's a problem, don't worry: He'll let you know, but He'll also help you get through it.

Let go of your laziness, and let God help you overcome it.

Slothfulness casts into a deep sleep, and an idle person will suffer hunger.
—PROVERBS 19:15 (ESV)

The Next Generation

IT'S AMAZING TO THINK we could write words that might spiritually affect someone halfway around the world. What about people yet to be born? Think of all those who have influenced millions of other people even though they passed on years and years ago. Jonathan Edwards, John and Charles Wesley, C. H. Spurgeon, Fanny Crosby, and Corrie ten Boom are just a few. Think and pray about what God would have you do to reach future generations, and then get busy!

Let go of thinking you have no impact, and let God show what a difference you can make.

Let this be written for a generation to come, so that a people yet to be created may praise the LORD.

—PSALM 102:18 (ESV)

Little versus Big

WE'VE ALL HEARD the phrase "little white lie." There's no such thing. A lie is a lie, and in God's eyes lying is a sin. As humans we tend to categorize sin. A lie is not as bad as cheating on our husband, which is not as bad as murder. But you know something? In God's eyes, sin is sin. One sin is not worse than another. All of those sins, even the "little white lies," caused Him to die on the cross and take our punishment. The cost for each of our sins, no matter how big or small, was Christ's life.

Let go of thinking your little sins don't matter, and let God take away all of them.

If we say we have no sin, we deceive ourselves,
and the truth is not in us.

—1 JOHN 1:8 (ESV)

Discovering Boldness

WHAT EXACTLY DOES IT MEAN to be bold for God? We should be loving and not afraid to share the Gospel. People need to know that God loves them and that He will forgive them of their sins if they repent. How can we be bold without turning people away from Him? This is where love comes in. When you have a conversation with someone, it should feel natural to work God into the conversation, because He has done so much for you that you're overwhelmed.

Let go of any timidity, and let God give you a boldness you didn't know you possessed.

And also for me, that words may be given to me in opening my mouth boldly to proclaim the mystery of the gospel.

—Ephesians 6:19 (ESV)

Hidden Mysteries

SOME PEOPLE GO through their entire lives wondering what their spiritual purpose is. God never meant it to be a secret. His plan is not hidden from us. Sure, there are times He uses us without our knowing—we don't get underfoot that way! No matter who we are or what we've done, God can use us. The apostle Paul was "the chief of sinners," yet when God caught hold of him, he took the Great Commission to heart. That's what's important.

Let go of thinking He is hiding your purpose, and let God make His purpose for you plain.

And to bring to light for everyone what is the plan of the mystery hidden for ages in God, who created all things.
—EPHESIANS 3:9 (ESV)

Following Our Fathers

THERE ARE MANY FATHERS in the Bible, but one sticks out as being so opposite from what God intends—Lot. He took his family to an ungodly place without thought for their protection. Then, when the girls had no marriage prospects, they got Lot drunk so they could sleep with him and become pregnant. You can't expect much of them since they'd only seen low moral standards. But no matter what your father was like, you have a heavenly Father who loves you.

Let go of any imperfect earthly father, and let God be the Father you follow.

Fathers, do not provoke your children to anger,
but bring them up in the discipline and
instruction of the Lord.
—EPHESIANS 6:4 (ESV)

A Parent's Responsibilities

IN EXODUS 2 we see a perfect example of what a mother's responsibilities are to her children. A mother protects her child, puts her child's best interests first, and provides what her child needs, not necessarily what her child wants. None of us will ever be a perfect parent. But we can be the best parent possible, and as with all things, God will help us along that journey as well.

Let go of trying to be the ideal parent in the world's eyes, and let God and His ideal for the perfect parent be the goal you strive to reach.

When she could hide him no longer, she took for him a basket made of bulrushes and daubed it with bitumen and pitch. She put the child in it and placed it among the reeds by the river bank.

—Exodus 2:3 (ESV)

The Ultimate Guide

A GUIDE IS SOMEONE who helps the inexperienced navigate. Guides are found almost anywhere, whether in the form of a person or a map. They can help us hike through the woods, experience a museum, or find our way home. God is the ultimate Guide. He guides us through this life on a daily basis. He helps us get through tough times and walks along beside us when the road is easy. He provided us with a handbook—the Bible—to instruct us even more. With a Guide like God, what do we have to fear?

Let go of your trepidation when walking along the road of life, and let God be your Guide.

That this is God, our God forever and ever.
He will guide us forever.
—PSALM 48:14 (ESV)

God's Provision

THE STORY OF THE EXODUS is amazing. God provided for the Israelites each step of the way. Someone actually did the math on the manna God provided. In order to feed the approximately one million Israelites, God needed to provide 4,500 tons of manna. Per day. For forty years. If you can comprehend that, you should have no trouble realizing that God can provide whatever it is you need.

Let go of finite thinking when it comes to Him, and let God prove Himself to you over and over again.

This is what the LORD has commanded: "Gather of it, each one of you, as much as he can eat. You shall each take an omer, according to the number of the persons that each of you has in his tent."
—EXODUS 16:16 (ESV)

Looking at God

SO MANY PEOPLE are all about the blessings they can receive from God, but then they get upset that God is not blessing, or at least not blessing where they see it. When we focus only on the blessing, we miss the point. We should be focusing on God. God's face will only shine upon ours when we are looking directly at Him. When we are turned in another direction, He only sees our back. If you want God's blessings to shine upon you, focus on Him. You will suddenly notice many little blessings popping up.

Let go of an earthly focus, and let God's face shine on yours when you look in His direction.

The Lord make his face to shine upon
you and be gracious to you.
—Numbers 6:25 (ESV)

Figureheads of Faith

WE ALL NEED SOMEONE to look up to. Many of us look up to our parents or grandparents, but unfortunately some of us lost those important people too young. The good news: God always has us covered, no matter what the circumstances. He provides examples who pop into our lives exactly when we need them. He knows what we need and He provides it. He does it simply because He loves us. That's our God.

Let go of believing you have no one to look up to, and let God open your eyes to see whom He has placed in your life.

Without counsel plans fail, but with
many advisers they succeed.
—Proverbs 15:22 (ESV)

Words That Lift

HOW MANY TIMES are you tempted, even eager, to say something negative? If people have a bad experience with a product, they have no qualms about leaving a bad review. But what about all the positive things that quickly pass through your mind and don't get said? Maybe we need to give some of those not only a second thought but a voice as well. Saying something uplifting can brighten a person's day. Maybe God put that thought in your mind at that moment because she needed to hear it.

Let go of dismissing positive thoughts, and let God use you to lift up someone else.

Let no corrupting talk come out of your mouths, but only such as is good for building up, as fits the occasion, that it may give grace to those who hear.

—Ephesians 4:29 (ESV)

Identity as a Woman

PEOPLE CAN MAKE IT SOUND like it's horrible to be a woman, but it's truly a gift from God. Part of being a woman can include being a daughter, a sister, a helpmeet to a husband, a mother, and an aunt. Those roles are blessings and identities given by God. According to the Bible, men and women were created unique to meet different needs. Praise God He has a purpose for each of us!

Let go of always trying to be something you're not, and let God show you the blessings He has for you as you are.

So God created man in his own image, in the image of God he created him; male and female he created them.
—GENESIS 1:27 (ESV)

Test with God's Help

WE AS CHRISTIANS need to have much discernment. To paraphrase C. H. Spurgeon, we need to watch out for the "almost right." Some things in the world are blatantly sinful. But what about those ideas that are so close to Christianity yet have one minor (or major) flaw? It's those flaws we need to watch out for. The only way we can truly be aware of what is right and wrong is to look to God. Study His words. Pray. Remain close to Him. If you question anything, seek Him for the answers you need.

Let go of believing everything you hear, and let God test those ideas with His Word.

Beloved, do not believe every spirit, but test the spirits to see whether they are from God, for many false prophets have gone out into the world.

—1 JOHN 4:1 (ESV)

Defining Moments

TWO PEOPLE CAN DEAL so differently with major health issues. For one of them, her disease defines who she is. Everything is all about her and her sickness. The other is the opposite. She uses her illness to bring glory to God by sharing how much He has brought her through. We all have defining moments. We need to choose whether that moment will be who we are or just become a part of us. Are you divorced or a single parent? Have you been in an accident that left you altered in appearance? Don't *be* that divorce or accident. Be who God intended you to be.

Let go of defining yourself by what's happened to you, and let God define you.

Come and hear, all you who fear God, and
I will tell what he has done for my soul.
—Psalm 66:16 (ESV)

Shameless Sharing

SOCIAL MEDIA is a great way to keep up with friends and family, especially those who are far away. It's also a great way to see people's true colors, how they really live. Unfortunately, many Christians have fallen into the trap. They post pictures and make comments that aren't Christlike. They check in at places they shouldn't be. And they have no shame. They don't care who knows. Swearing, barhopping, and revealing photos should not be part of a Christian's life. Yes, everyone makes mistakes once in a while, but repeated behavior that's shown off in pride is not God's way.

Let go of shameful ways, and let God help you when you come before Him repentant.

Everyone who makes a practice of sinning also practices lawlessness; sin is lawlessness.

—1 John 3:4 (ESV)

The Perfect Mediator

THERE MAY BE TIMES when you feel you need a mediator. What you're trying to say isn't coming out as you planned and misunderstandings abound. Mediators are often found in the court systems and act as go-betweens. Did you know we have our very own Mediator? The Son will go to the Father on our behalf. We can go to God the Father ourselves, but what a feeling to know that Jesus does as well! The best part is that Jesus knows our hearts, and He knows what's best for us.

Let go of facing problems alone, and let God listen to His Son on your behalf.

For there is one God, and there is one mediator between God and men, the man Christ Jesus.

—1 TIMOTHY 2:5 (ESV)

Held Accountable

AS CHRISTIANS we are held to a higher standard, and we need to hold each other accountable. True believers want to know when they aren't measuring up. They want to know where they're lacking so they can change and better themselves. Find some accountability partners to help you. Make sure these are godly people who hold the same values you do. Don't nitpick each other, but pray for each other daily. Kindly give advice when necessary. Most of all, love each other as Christ loves you.

Let go of neglecting the value of accountability, and let God bring godly friends into your life who will help sharpen you.

Iron sharpens iron, and one man sharpens another.
—Proverbs 27:17 (ESV)

Inevitable Conflict

CONFLICT IS A FACT of life we all must deal with occasionally, even among Christians. Or maybe *especially* among Christians. So many of us would rather be fake or insincere than face a conflict, but it's much preferable to approach that conflict head-on. We all have different personalities; because of that, we won't agree all the time. If you do have to approach someone about a conflict, put the matter to prayer first. Ask God to give you the words to say in love. Writing down your thoughts so you stay on topic can also be helpful.

Let go of letting conflict continue, and let God help you find a resolution.

Be angry and do not sin; do not let the sun go down on your anger.
—EPHESIANS 4:26 (ESV)

Watching the Weak

HURT PEOPLE ARE often vulnerable. Others seek these vulnerable people out, prey on them, and take advantage whenever they can. We not only need to make sure we don't become victims, but we also need to watch out for those who are weaker. New Christians are especially vulnerable to the ways of the world. Satan works subtly. When one is not strong in the faith and lacks knowledge of solid doctrine, it's easy to be led astray. Remember, you didn't start out strong; be there for others who are where you once were.

Let go of being a predator, and let God turn you into a protector.

Rescue the weak and the needy; deliver them from the hand of the wicked.

—PSALM 82:4 (ESV)

Unity in Christ

WITH SO MANY PEOPLE a part of the body of Christ, with so many diverse personalities, cultures, and experiences, it's a wonder we could be unified about anything. We can hardly be on the same page of an issue when we're all in the same physical church building, let alone the entire world. But most of the things we aren't unified on have no relevance to salvation. The paint color of our sanctuaries doesn't matter. Whether we wear dresses or jeans doesn't matter. What matters are our hearts and that we have accepted Christ as our personal Savior.

Let go of petty differences within your church, and let God open your eyes to what matters.

How good and pleasant it is when God's people live together in unity!

—Psalm 133:1 (NIV)

Prayer Before Confrontation

CONFRONTATION IS NOT A JOB in which anyone really enjoys taking part. Gathering up the courage to confront someone is just as difficult as the hurtful words that are often said. Before any confronting can be done, you must seek wisdom from God in prayer. It would be wise to seek advice from other believers and have them pray over the situation as well. When a situation is bathed in prayer, the outcome may not be as tragic as you thought it would be.

Let go of the fear of confrontation, and let God take care of the situation before you even begin.

If your brother sins against you, go and tell him his fault, between you and him alone.

—Matthew 18:15a (ESV)

A True Relationship

HAVE YOU EVER been disappointed with someone? You're not alone. We have great expectations for new relationships. The interaction may go well for a while, but then suddenly the relationship can turn sour if the person turns out to be the complete opposite of whom you expected. The disillusionment can be heartbreaking. But God is never false. He can't be. Unlike humans, God will never fail us. Look to Him when you don't feel you can look to anyone else.

Let go of fake relationships, and let God build a relationship with you like you never had before.

But Jesus on his part did not entrust himself to them, because he knew all people and needed no one to bear witness about man, for he himself knew what was in man.
—JOHN 2:24-25 (ESV)

The Value of Trust

TRUST IS A TRAIT in people that can be hard to come by. When trust has been lost, it can take a lifetime to regain it. But you have the power to make sure you are trustworthy. You can be where you say you'll be. You can do what you said you'd do. If we can't be trusted with the small things. how will anyone feel they can trust us with bigger things? That goes not only for our earthly life but also for our spiritual life. Trust is a trait of our heavenly Father that we need to emulate.

Let go of your distrust of people, and let God grow you into a trustworthy person.

A gracious woman gets honor, and violent men get riches.
—PROVERBS 11:16 (ESV)

Never Stop Growing

A SMALL CHILD once determined he was going to read his Bible and pray every day so he could "grow, grow, grow," like the song he sang in church said. He wanted to be tall. Spiritually, the only way we will grow and stay close to God is through daily prayer and Bible study. We can be saved but still not know God. Growing in a relationship with Him is the only way we can accomplish that.

Let go of your stunted spiritual growth, and let God show you all He has to offer.

Practice these things, immerse yourself in them, so that all may see your progress.
—1 TIMOTHY 4:15 (ESV)

Thought Life

A PERSON'S THOUGHT LIFE can be deceiving. How many times have you supposedly been listening to someone, yet your thoughts were a million miles away? Our minds can quickly wander to places they have no business being. Have you ever had a negative or potentially hurtful thought about a friend? Have you ever thought about someone other than your spouse in a way you shouldn't? The Bible tells us to think on things that are pure, admirable, and lovely. Focus on those types of thoughts.

Let go of thoughts that are displeasing to the Lord, and let God fill your mind.

We destroy arguments and every lofty opinion raised against the knowledge of God, and take every thought captive to obey Christ.

—2 CORINTHIANS 10:5 (ESV)

Complete in God

HAVE YOU EVER KNOWN a woman who couldn't seem to live without a man—or vice versa? Some of us are afraid to be alone. Some feel incomplete without a partner by our side. Fortunately, there is One who can complete us. His name is Jesus Christ. If we are not settled within ourselves or don't have a fulfilling relationship with God, no relationship will be successful. We need to look to God to fulfill our needs and trust in Him to send the perfect spouse to fulfill our earthly needs.

Let go of the idea that any ordinary partner can complete you, and let God fill all the empty spaces of your life.

By this we know that we abide in him and he in us,
because he has given us of his Spirit.
—1 John 4:13 (ESV)

Reflections of Love

IF YOU'RE MARRIED, how you act reflects on your spouse. Yet some people behave in ways that cause others to talk and look poorly on their spouse. No spouse is perfect, but that's not for us to judge. We can only control our own actions. In our marriage, our walk should be blameless. There should be no reason for others to doubt our intentions or actions. Be a godly spouse and leave that as a reflection on your partner.

Let go of any questionable behavior on your part, and let God reflect on you and in turn your spouse.

Their wives likewise must be dignified, not slanderers, but sober-minded, faithful in all things.

—1 TIMOTHY 3:11 (ESV)

God's Team

IN HIGH SCHOOL and college, students are given group activities that help build teamwork. Service for the Lord often requires teamwork. We need teamwork to hold us up in prayer, to tag-team us when we're weary, or simply to work together to make the load lighter. Some might plant a seed in someone's heart, where another might reap the harvest of salvation. We need each other. Besides, working alongside a friend is much more fun than working alone.

Let go of trying to save the world on your own, and let God provide you with good teammates.

Two are better than one, because they have a good reward for their toil. For if they fall, one will lift up his fellow. But woe to him who is alone when he falls and has not another to lift him up!

—ECCLESIASTES 4:9–10 (ESV)

The Gift of Reconciliation

RECONCILIATION CAN BE difficult, especially between family members. There was once a mother and daughter who were in conflict. When the mother passed away, the daughter carried an overwhelming sense of guilt. Years later, another woman told the daughter that her mother had forgiven her. That was all the daughter needed to hear. As sinners, we have turned our backs on God; it is our choice whether we reconcile with Him or not. Christ paid all our debts and has forgiven us. We just need to turn to Him and accept Him.

Let go of burdens, and let God bring you into a relationship with Him.

For if while we were enemies we were reconciled to God by the death of his Son, much more, now that we are reconciled, shall we be saved by his life.

—ROMANS 5:10 (ESV)

A New Prayer

"I DON'T FEEL LIKE IT." There are many aspects of life we may not feel like doing what must be done. If you don't feel like working, your employer may not feel like paying. When people say they don't feel like praying, that's exactly the time they need to pray. Instead of sitting down and saying a traditional-style prayer, try something new. Journal your feelings. Write a letter to God. Sit outside in a quiet place and open your heart wordlessly to Him. Open the lines of communication somehow and know God will respond.

Let go of your reluctance to pray, and let God take His place in your heart and mind.

The LORD is near to all who call on him,
to all who call on him in truth.
—PSALM 145:18 (ESV)

Finding Ourselves

IT'S NOT UNUSUAL for people to spend a lifetime finding themselves. Have you ever known a career student who gets one degree after another? The problem some people struggle with when "finding themselves" is that it's not about trying to figure out who they want to be, but discovering who God created them to be. Only when we change our perspective will our lives fall into place.

Let go of finding yourself, and let God show you who He created you to be.

For by the grace given to me I say to everyone among you not to think of himself more highly than he ought to think, but to think with sober judgment, each according to the measure of faith that God has assigned.

—ROMANS 12:3 (ESV)

Grateful Is Good

WHEN WE FOCUS on the grateful, it helps us in more ways than we can imagine. When we're so focused on the positive, the negative thoughts get squeezed out. Our positivity increases the more we entertain grateful thoughts. Fear will often disappear, because we learn to trust in God. Abundance appears because we open our eyes to it. Start and end your day with grateful thoughts and feelings, and try to fit in a few more throughout the day.

Let go of negative thoughts that cloud your mind, and let God and His goodness fill you with gratitude.

Give thanks in all circumstances; for this is the will of God in Christ Jesus for you.
—1 Thessalonians 5:18 (ESV)

Overcoming Failure

EVERY DAY WE STRUGGLE with failure. But God knows we will fail; He even expects it. God knows what we're made of—dust. Dust is nothing. In spite of our failures, God still loves us and has compassion for us. Knowing that can help us want to work even harder to overcome our failures. We know that we may never completely succeed. But that's OK, because we also know He will help us. We're His beloved children.

Let go of your failures, give them to Him, and let God love you, imperfections and all.

For he knows how we are formed,
he remembers that we are dust.
—PSALM 103:14 (NIV)

Empty Traditions

WE THINK A LOT about traditions during holiday seasons. We often do the same things our families did when we were children, because it would not feel like the holiday without those traditions. Some traditions are healthy, but others we need to break or make anew. There are countless people who go to church simply because that's what their parents did. They go, sit in a pew, and leave without ever having been touched by the Holy Spirit. Don't make your religion only about tradition. Grow closer to God by building a personal relationship with Him.

Let go of meaningless traditions, and let God build a relationship with you.

See to it that no one takes you captive by philosophy and empty deceit, according to human tradition, according to the elemental spirits of the world, and not according to Christ.
—COLOSSIANS 2:8 (ESV)

Deeper Devotion

WHEN WE FIRST ACCEPT Christ as our Savior, everything is new and exciting. If we're not careful, the Christian life can seem mundane as time goes by. The cure: we need to grow in our commitment to Him. We must worship Him daily, not just within the confines of the church building. We need to spend our quiet time in fellowship with God, building a personal relationship with Him. We must obey when He tests us and keep Him as the focal point of our lives.

Let go of any rut in your relationship with your Savior, and let God develop His character in you.

But the steadfast love of the LORD is from everlasting to everlasting on those who fear him, and his righteousness to children's children.

—PSALM 103:17 (ESV)

Set Free

WE STRUGGLE TO DEAL with a myriad of emotions on a daily basis, such as fear, anxiety, worry, shame, and neglect. Unfortunately, sometimes we allow those emotions to take over our lives, leaving us in a sort of bondage. But as with many things in life, God gave us examples in the Bible to help us express our emotions in a healthy and beneficial way. Many of these passages are Psalms. It's a comfort to know that others have gone before us in similar situations and have come through. With God's help, we will move forward as well.

Let go of the bondage that holds you captive, and let God set your heart free.

Out of my distress I called on the LORD; the LORD answered me and set me free.
—PSALM 118:5 (ESV)

Angels on Earth

IT'S THE LITTLE THINGS we do in life that can make the biggest difference, not only in our lives but also in the lives of others. Everyone can be an angel on earth to someone in need, and it all starts with one little act of kindness from ordinary people, doing ordinary things, but getting extraordinary results with drastically changed lives. It could be as simple as buying someone lunch, returning a wallet, or being friendly.

Let go of thinking you need to do a lot to make a big difference, and let God open your eyes to the little ways you can be someone's angel.

Do not neglect to do good and to share what you have,
for such sacrifices are pleasing to God.
—HEBREWS 13:6 (ESV)

Beyond Betrayal

PEOPLE DON'T OFTEN ASK others "Have you been betrayed?" The answer is more than likely "Yes." Betrayal is so rampant in this world, and it hurts. Betrayal can lead to broken relationships, unforgiveness, and bitterness. People who have been betrayed often become betrayers later in life. Greed, selfishness, and a whole host of other factors can also lead to betrayal. God knows all about betrayal. It began even before the creation of the earth, with an angel named Lucifer. One can either live in the aftermath of betrayal or use it to become a better, not bitter, person.

Let go of the effects of betrayal on your life, and let God heal your heart.

Even my close friend in whom I trusted, who ate my bread, has lifted his heel against me.

—Psalm 41:9 (ESV)

Simple Christianity

CHRISTIANITY CAN SOMETIMES be confusing for nonbelievers. Everyone has likely heard preachers who use one huge vocabulary word after another, making it almost impossible to follow. But the message of the Gospel is simple: we are sinners. God loved us and chose to die on the cross and take the punishment for our sin. All we have to do is accept the salvation He freely gives. We don't need to live a perfect life—we can't do that anyway.

Let go of complicating the Gospel message, and let God give you the words to keep it simple for even the youngest child to understand.

In this is love, not that we have loved God but that he loved us and sent his Son to be the propitiation for our sins.

—1 JOHN 4:10 (ESV)

His Hope

HOPE IS A LITTLE WORD with big meaning. There is life in that word. No matter what your situation is or what you've done, there is always hope. Suffering comes to everyone sometime. In the midst of trouble, it's difficult to see if God knows what we're going through. But there is hope—God knows and cares. If you're in a time of hopelessness, use this time wisely. Journal about your thoughts and feelings. Write down Scriptures that offer insight. Later, when your hope is restored, you will be able to look back and see how far God brought you and how He worked in your life.

Let go of thinking there is no hope, and let God restore hope in His time.

Rejoice in hope, be patient in tribulation, be constant in prayer.
—ROMANS 12:12 (ESV)

"If Only. . ."

SO MANY TIMES in life, we look back with regret and say, "If only. . ." But change that "If only" statement into a "What if" question. In a matter of seconds, you have gone from negative to positive and found a goal for the future. Turning those "if only" regrets of the past into "what if" suggestions, with God's help, can make our dreams come true and change our life and the lives of others around us.

Let go of thinking it's too late to change, and let God change your perspective when He says, "What if. . ."

And to put on the new self, created after the likeness of God in true righteousness and holiness.
—EPHESIANS 4:24 (ESV)

Walking When It's Dark

DARKNESS IS a universal experience, yet many people still fear it. The "dark" is what we perceive as bad or scary. Unfortunately, not all darkness can be solved with a simple flashlight. But know that darkness, both spiritual and physical, can be a time when God speaks to us. God told Abraham to count the stars to find the number of his descendants. Jacob wrestled with God all night long. These nighttime experiences brought these men closer to God. The Israelites left Egypt in the dark of night, beginning an entirely new life for them. God will be there for us during our dark times.

Let go of walking in the dark, and let God speak to you in the quiet.

Even the darkness is not dark to you; the night is bright as the day, for darkness is as light with you.
—Psalm 139:12 (ESV)

Religion or Relationship?

WHEN WE HEAR the word *religious*, it's not always in a good connotation. People's perspectives on religion can be a great divider—coming between families and friendships instead of opening the door for meaningful conversation. One might call someone else religious in a negative sense, as if he's been brainwashed into his beliefs. One might say a person has no religion. Yet religion is simply one's belief system, so everyone has some sort of religion. Just don't let your religion take the place of a relationship with Christ.

Let go of religion, and let God be a witness to deeper relationship through you.

If anyone thinks he is religious and does not bridle his tongue but deceives his heart, this person's religion is worthless.

—JAMES 1:26 (ESV)

The Glory of God

SOME DEFINITIONS OF GLORY include the ideas of fame and renown. But when we think of God's glory, it is more His presence in our lives. The Israelites had the presence, or the glory, of God with them as a cloud by day and a pillar of fire by night as they wandered through the dessert. We may not have those things, but we can see and feel God's glorious presence in our lives as He works in us and through us. God's glory can change lives.

Let go of trying to see His glor in the lives of others, and let God give you the experience for yourself.

And we all, with unveiled face, beholding the glory of the Lord, are being transformed into the same image from one degree of glory to another.

—2 Corinthians 3:18a (ESV)

Greater Expectations

EVERYONE HAS MOMENTS of feeling incapable, overwhelmed, and insecure, but some people live with those debilitating feelings constantly. And then there's the pretense that everything is OK, which is exhausting. Satan is the father of lies, and often it is he who puts those thoughts of insecurity in our minds and hearts. Even knowing that, letting go is extremely challenging. Sometimes the expectations that cause us to feel like we aren't enough come from others; other times, they are self-induced expectations, with little nudges from that father of lies. But God can help us deal with our insecurities, no matter where they originate.

Let go of living up to the demands of others, and let God's expectations be your goal.

My soul, wait thou only upon God; for my expectation is from him.

—Psalm 62:5 (KJV)

A Need to Refuel

MANY CHRISTIANS have gotten so caught up in serving God that they have moved away from having a personal relationship with Him. Sometimes, like Martha in the Bible, we choose simple serving over actually spending time with God—whether through prayer, Bible study, listening for His voice, or seeking His presence. Our priorities often get turned around or misplaced. We need to maintain a loving and meaningful relationship with God and not be so busy running around serving Him that we burn ourselves out. Take time to refuel yourself.

Let go of always running to serve, and let God serve you as you sit at His feet.

You and the people with you will certainly wear yourselves out, for the thing is too heavy for you. You are not able to do it alone.
—Exodus 18:18 (ESV)

What's Missing?

MANY PEOPLE LOOK for happiness in stuff. Society tells us we deserve everything we want. But think about the story of the rich, young ruler in the Bible who couldn't let go of all of his belongings to follow Christ. We don't have to give up everything we own, but maybe we should examine our lives and get rid of all the things that detract from what makes life worth living. We can live with less and regain true happiness.

Let go of all the stuff that keeps you from enjoying life, and let God show you what you've been missing.

And Jesus, looking at him, loved him, and said to him, "You lack one thing: go, sell all that you have and give to the poor, and you will have treasure in heaven; and come, follow me."

—MARK 10:21 (ESV)

God's Company

TO SOME IT MAY SEEM almost ridiculous that God, the Creator of the universe, actually wants to spend time with us. But that's exactly the case. He is our Father and that is the kind of relationship He wants to have with us. Worship is one way we can build our relationship with the Lord. He doesn't need our worship; He just wants us to show our desire for a relationship with Him. Relationships are two-sided; we must seek Him out. We can make memories with God just as we can with our earthly families.

Let go of anything that keeps you from having a relationship with Him, and let God become your number-one priority.

The Lord your God is in your midst, a mighty one who will save; he will rejoice over you with gladness; he will quiet you by his love; he will exult over you with loud singing.

—Zephaniah 3:17 (ESV)

Your Love Story

THE GREATEST COMMANDMENT is for us to love God with all of our heart, soul, and mind. We need to follow that by loving those around us as we love ourselves. So many people are content to show up at church Sunday morning and not give a thought to God or others the rest of the week. But there is one very simple way to love others around us every day: share the Gospel. You don't need to be a scholar; you just need to be willing. You don't have to go to a foreign country; just step out your front door and share your story.

Let go of thinking you have nothing to share, tell your story, and let God bring about miracles in your neighbors.

You shall love your neighbor as yourself.

—MATTHEW 22:39B (ESV)

The Trinity

WHEN TEACHING CHILDREN about the Trinity, we may offer them an example such as, "I am a wife, a mother, and a sister. I am always the same person, yet depending on how one sees me, the role I play will vary." The idea of the Trinity can be challenging. Yet there are clues to the Trinity throughout the Bible and creation. We just have to look. God is in everything and He can be seen in everything if we only open our eyes.

Let go of trying to understand the technical Trinity, and let God the Father, Son, and Holy Spirit reveal themselves to you in their own ways.

According to the foreknowledge of God the Father, in the sanctification of the Spirit, for obedience to Jesus Christ and for sprinkling with his blood: May grace and peace be multiplied to you.
—1 PETER 1:12 (ESV)

Freedom from Evil

EVIL IS COMMON in today's world, specifically when dealing with pride, bitterness, greed, lust, the mind, and past wounds. Even Christians are not immune to the effects of evil. Evil can influence even the strongest of us. Because of evil, we all have sin in our lives, from which only Christ can free us. We need to identify the areas in our lives where we have given Satan a foothold. Is there some sin committed repeatedly in spite of a desire to stop? Determine what evil snares are holding you back, then find freedom in God.

Let go of any evil ways you may have, and let God provide freedom that you've never known before.

Live as people who are free, not using your freedom as a cover-up for evil, but living as servants of God.

—1 PETER 2:16 (ESV)

Not Offended

IN A WORLD where people seem to be offended at the least little thing, we can all choose to not be offended. We can choose to not let anger and resentment be a part of our everyday lives. Although anger is a natural part of our emotions, it's how and when we react in that anger that is important. We can choose to love, forgive, and see people as they could be, not necessarily as they are. After all, no one is perfect. You often hear stories of murderers being forgiven by the families of the victim. These extraordinary people get what it means to not be offended.

Let go of the hurt someone may have caused you, and let God make a difference in his life.

For the sake of Christ, then, I am content with weaknesses, insults, hardships, persecutions, and calamities. For when I am weak, then I am strong.

—2 CORINTHIANS 12:10 (ESV)

Spiritual Warfare

MOVIES, TV SHOWS, and books have given many people a skewed version of angels, demons, and even Satan himself, making them even more vulnerable to spiritual attacks. Is heaven real? Is hell real? Is spiritual warfare real? Of course, to see the unseen world one has to be a true follower of Jesus Christ. Most believers know that spiritual warfare is real and that we are in a constant battle. Faith, prayer, and knowledge of the Scriptures are all part of fighting the unseen battle we face on a daily basis.

Let go of looking to nonbelievers for spiritual answers, and let God provide the answers.

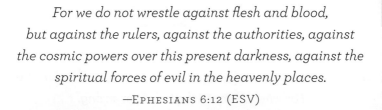

For we do not wrestle against flesh and blood, but against the rulers, against the authorities, against the cosmic powers over this present darkness, against the spiritual forces of evil in the heavenly places.
—EPHESIANS 6:12 (ESV)

God's Goals

"BUCKET LISTS" (of things we want to do before we die) are becoming more and more popular. There is nothing wrong with having dreams and goals. The problem comes when bucket lists are created from a human mindset. Are you looking to have a more fulfilling and spiritually goal-oriented life? What if we created a bucket list from God's perspective? Some spiritually minded things God might add: building a strong foundation that can withstand storms, putting others first, finding true joy in God, being an overcomer, loving our neighbors, and many more.

Let go of your ideas, and let God create a list of goals for you to accomplish.

And the LORD answered me: "Write the vision; make it plain on tablets, so he may run who reads it."
—HABAKKUK 2:2 (ESV)

Finding a Lifeline

SOME PEOPLE THINK the life of a Christian should be easy—that the moment we accept Him as Savior, all problems cease. This "easy street" concept couldn't be further from the truth. We are still a fallen people living in a fallen world. Bad things happen—whether the pain is physical, emotional, or mental. But there are also times when that pain comes from God for discipline—such as shifting our focus back on Him, learning patience, or prompting prayer. Wherever our pain comes from, we can see God's grace and goodness and be confident that He is our Lifeline while we are going through difficult times.

Let go of wondering why bad things happen, and let God teach you as you hold on to Him.

For the Lord disciplines the one he loves, and chastises every son whom he receives.
—HEBREWS 12:6 (ESV)

A Song in Your Heart

EVER FIND A SONG that worships God suddenly on your heart? It's there because of Him. Our hearts on their own are "desperately wicked" (Jeremiah 17:9 KJV). You've probably also had thoughts pop into your head that made you wonder, *Where did that evil come from?* Those thoughts come from Satan trying to push out thoughts of God. If we're not careful, he could be successful. To combat Satan, fill your mind with wholesome, God-centered music, books, movies, and other influences. There's truth behind the saying, "garbage in, garbage out."

Let go of putting unrighteous visions into your mind, and let God fill your every thought.

But none says, "Where is God my Maker,
who gives songs in the night?"
—JOB 25:10 (ESV)

Longing for Holiness

HAVE YOU EVER been mocked by someone calling you holy? Maybe it's because you go to church. Maybe it's because you choose not to participate in certain activities. That person is actually giving you a compliment because she sees Christ in you. God is the only One who is truly holy. We can never hope to attain perfect holiness, but that doesn't mean we can't try. Because God is holy He deserves our worship. One day all will fall before Him since He is the Almighty and Creator of everything.

Let go of the hurtful words people use against you, and let God's holiness shine through you as you worship Him.

Holy, holy, holy, is the Lord God Almighty, who was and is and is to come!

—REVELATION 4:8B (ESV)

Sovereign Over All

WE OFTEN HEAR that God is sovereign, but what exactly does that mean? A dictionary definition might include the words *greatest, superior, supreme, authority. Sovereign* means that God is the ruler of all. In short, God is in control. There is nothing that happens in our lives that He doesn't know about. However, God is not the cause of all the bad things that happen to us; human free will made those decisions on its own. But because God is sovereign, He can take anything and turn it around for our good.

Let go of thinking you're in control, and let God work His way in your life.

The LORD has established his throne in the heavens, and his kingdom rules over all.
—PSALM 103:19 (ESV)

New Opportunities

HAVE YOU EVER wondered why you were born in the time and place you were? Why this continent, country, state, or city? God placed you exactly where He wanted and needed you to be. Every day is a new opportunity to serve Him, no matter where you are. Service to our Lord is why we are here on earth. Do you keep your eyes open for these opportunities every day to share a word, a smile, a hug, or the Gospel with someone in need?

Let go of fretting because of your location, and let God open the doors of opportunity right where you are.

Making the most of every opportunity, because the days are evil.

—Ephesians 5:16 (NIV)

Inviting Him In

IF YOU LIVE in a house with others, strife is inevitable from time to time. There may be periods of discord in your family. When this happens, have you ever thought about inviting Christ to your home? Take some time to pray in each room of your home. Pray for each member individually as you move through their personal spaces, and for family unity as a whole in common areas.

Let go of the strife that hangs in the atmosphere of your home, and let God's presence enter and stay.

The LORD's curse is on the house of the wicked,
but he blesses the home of the righteous.
—Proverbs 3:33 (NIV)

The Posture of Prayer

SOME PEOPLE KNEEL to pray. Some prostrate themselves. Some close their eyes. Some leave them open. Some pray long prayers. Some keep them short. Some people get too caught up in all of the above. What matters when we pray is our hearts. Kneeling is fine if you have time for a longer prayer and if you have the physical strength to do it. Short prayers are fine along with open eyes if you're driving down the road and see a reminder to pray for a friend.

Let go of human and physical mechanics of prayer, and let God tell you when, where, and how to pray as He nudges your heart.

Come, let us bow down in worship, let us kneel before the LORD our Maker.
—PSALM 95:6 (NIV)

Standing True

THERE WAS ONCE a couple whose daughter watched and took note of when they stood up for what was right. Their friends may have been getting drunk, but they refused to even take a sip. The father was bullied and fired from his job when he refused take part in financial shenanigans. The mother never joined conversations in which women talked provocatively about other men. Parents can be wonderful examples of how to stand true when others around cave to sin. Know that people are watching you as well.

Let go of fitting in with the crowd, and let God give you the strength to stand strong and true.

So whoever knows the right thing to do and fails to do it, for him it is sin.

—JAMES 4:17 (ESV)

A New Dawn

FOR THE PAST YEAR we have practiced letting go of tiresome ways or things of the world that bring us down. Hopefully, letting go of the unnecessary thoughts, feelings, and time-consumers has become a habit by now. Hopefully, you've grown closer to God throughout the year. Tomorrow is a new dawn, a new day, full of new opportunities to show the love of Christ to those with whom you come in contact. Teach others what you've learned about letting go and fully trusting in and depending on God. Continue to seek first His kingdom, and everything else will fall into place.

Don't let go of letting go of things that are detrimental to you, and continue to let God be the Lord and Master of your life.

But seek first the kingdom of God and his righteousness, and all these things will be added to you.
—Matthew 6:33 (ESV)